Possibility and Necessity

Volume 2
The Role of Necessity in Cognitive Development

The research reported in this volume was supported by the Fonds National Suisse de la Recherche Scientifique and the Ford Foundation.

Possibility and Necessity

Volume 2
The Role of Necessity in Cognitive Development

Jean Piaget

with
E. Ackermann-Valladao,
I. Berthoud-Papandropoulou,
A. Blanchet, A. Boder,
C. Brulhart, C. Coll,
D. de Capona, S. Dionnet,
A. Henriques-Christophides,
H. Kilcher, E. Marbach,
E. Marti, C. Monnier,
K. Noschis, E. Rappe-du-
Cher, J. Vauclair, and
R. Zubel

Translated from the French
by Helga Feider

University of Minnesota Press • Minneapolis

The University of Minnesota Press gratefully
acknowledges translation assistance provided for this
book by the French Ministry of Culture.

Originally published as *Le possible et le nécessaire, 2:
L'evolution du nécessaire chez l'enfant*, copyright ©
1983 by Presses Universitaires de France.

Published by the University of Minnesota Press,
2037 University Avenue Southeast, Minneapolis, MN
55414.
Published simultaneously in Canada
by Fitzhenry & Whiteside Limited, Markham.
Printed in the United States of America.

Library of Congress Cataloging-in-Publication Data
Piaget, Jean, 1896–
  Possibility and necessity.
  Translation of: Le possible et le nécessaire.
  Includes bibliographical references and indexes.
  Contents: v. 1. The role of possibility in cognitive
development — v. 2. The role of necessity in
cognitive development.
  1. Possibility—Psychological aspects. 2. Necessity
(Philosophy) 3. Reality—Psychological aspects.
4. Cognition in children. I. Title.
BF723.P67P5413 1987   155.4'13   86–7052
ISBN 0-8166-1372-9 (v. 2)
ISBN 0-8166-1370-2 (v. 1)

The University of Minnesota
is an equal-opportunity
educator and employer.

Contents

Volume 2
The Role of Necessity in Cognitive Development

Volume 1
The Role of Possibility in Cognitive Development

Possibility and Necessity

Volume 2
The Role of Necessity in Cognitive Development

Introduction

This second volume on possibility and necessity, which is devoted to the development of necessity in the child, was written by Piaget himself. Because he was pressed to complete various ongoing projects, he unfortunately did not have time to revise this manuscript and give it its final form. Commissioned by him to look after the editing of his manuscripts, I was able to count on the dedicated and competent collaboration of my colleagues Jean-Blaise Grize and François Bresson in reviewing the manuscript and clarifying certain parts in it.

By way of introduction, it seemed to me that I could best represent the thoughts of our master by reproducing and adapting the following extracts from a presentation he delivered at the 21st International Congress of Psychology in Paris in 1976.*

Bärbel Inhelder

In approaching the problem of necessity we do not intend to study modal logic, but rather to relate necessity, as we did possibility, to the development of the notion of *reality*.

Possibility has always appeared to us as being relative to a subject and not as preformed in reality. If in physics one speaks of "virtual work," etc., this concept gets constituted only in the mind of the physicist, and when a real transformation is interpreted as the actualization of a possibility, this only means that it was real from the start and also in its determinism, even if it was not at first observable. The same is true for necessity, which is a product of the subject's inferential compositions and is also not open to direct observation. What one gets by observation is only varying degrees of generality. Generality is not ne-

*I am grateful to Paul Fraisse for having given permission to draw on J. Piaget, "Le réel, le possible et le nécessaire," *Proceedings of the 21st International Congress of Psychology* (Paris: Presses Universitaires de France, 1978).

3

cessity, however, and where one is assimilated to the other we get *pseudo-necessities*.

Our research shows that the relations between possibility and necessity are complex and that there is interference between the two even in the initial stages: this raises an unexpected problem as to what young children consider as "real." Because of an initial lack of differentiation between the factual and the normative, reality—as interpreted by 4- to 5-year-old children—frequently appears as what an observer or more advanced subject would see as pseudonecessity or *pseudoimpossibility*. Incidentally, numerous examples of such pseudonecessities can be found, even in the history of the sciences.*

The development of necessity appears to parallel that of possibility. The initial forms consist in simple local necessities that result from elementary compositions observable at the end of the sensorimotor period and further developed in preoperational representation. At the concrete-operational stage we already find certain systematic types of necessity, such as recursiveness, transitivity, conservation, and so forth. Obviously, at the formal-operational stage, necessity becomes completely general. We hypothesize that there are various degrees of strength of necessity, related to what contemporary logicians call the *force* of structures. But what can one mean when speaking of the variable strength of different forms of necessity? We do not simply mean the number of necessary relations that a structure contains. We believe that there are also qualitative, *intensional* differences: comparing an analytical judgment such as identity, $n=n$, with a synthetic judgment like "any whole number is succeeded by another whole number, $n \rightarrow (n+1)$," we clearly see that the latter involves a greater number of relations, including order, equal intervals between n and $n+1$, and equivalence of units. But incorporating more relations is not only a matter of complexity or richness: because it consists in the union of distinct characteristics within a whole, this complexity requires a greater integrating force. In this sense, necessity appears to us as a measure of this integration. Similarly, possibility is an index of the richness of differentiation. This explains the parallelism in the development of the two.

In general, one might imagine a general law of development encompassing reality, possibility, and necessity. This law would specify three periods in their relations. The first is one of nondifferentiation: reality includes many pseudonecessities, whereas possibility consists in simple, direct extensions of actual realities.

The second period (coinciding with the formation of *groupings* and *concrete operations*) is one of differentiation of the three modalities: possibilities unfold into families of co-possibilities; necessity transcends the local coordinations,

---

*See J. Piaget and R. Garcia, *Psychogenèse et histoire des sciences* (Paris: Flammarion, 1983).

generating operational compositions determining the necessary forms; and reality consists in concrete contents.

The third period, finally, is one of integration of the three modalities within a total system so that reality appears to the subject as a set of actualizations among others that are possible. But it is simultaneously subordinated to systems of necessary connections.

Thus, it appears that reality is absorbed at either pole by possibility and necessity respectively, in a twofold subordination that also enriches it by assimilating it into the constructions and interpretations of the cognitive subject. This, however, should not be interpreted as an idealistic conclusion, for reasons that are linked to the general relation between subject and object. In fact, reality includes the subject as an organism who represents a physical object and is the center of continuous material actions from which the subject derives knowledge. In reciprocal fashion, the subject then incorporates reality by means of possibility and necessity—that is, by means of the actions that the subject *can* carry out and that, when coordinated, give rise to necessities.

One final remark is necessary to make clear the generality of the foregoing conclusions. We have assumed that possibility and necessity are relative to the subject only and are not given in the objects. At the same time, we grant that our organism is an object among others. We do not see any contradiction here, since every living thing, unlike inorganic matter, is at once subject and object, being the source of behaviors (this includes plant life, which also acts upon its environment). It is thus necessary to assume a biological *possible* and a biological *necessary*. These are indicated most evidently by the necessity for survival of conserving and entertaining relatively "normal" states and by the possibility of "abnormal" variations, as well as variations that lead to progress. Now, normality and abnormality have no meaning in physics (random fluctuations are of a different nature); but they may be considered as the organic source of cognitive *normativity*, relative to which possibility and necessity exist, as we have seen.

1

A Problem of Physical Necessity

with R. Zubel and E. Rappe du Cher

The nature of physical necessity raises the central question concerning the contributions of object and subject at different levels of development. Simply assuming, as did Aristotle, a "real" necessity that characterizes the objective connections between external events is problematic. Necessity is not directly observable but is always a product of deductive composition; and even in the case of connections considered causal, experience only furnishes regular successions: to go from this generalization to necessity, the subject's construction of a deductive model remains indispensable. On the other hand, it is not sufficient to equate such models simply with logico-mathematical structures, even if one only "attributes" their operations to the objects themselves, because it remains desirable to have as close a correspondence as possible between the necessary relations inherent in the subject's model and those to be attributed to the objects themselves (and which can only be approximated by the model). In other words, it is desirable to guarantee a certain isomorphism between the model and the necessities assumed to exist within the objects. In this respect, we will demonstrate the mediating role of space; in addition, we will consider what in physics are called *principles* (conservations, symmetries, etc.), which express what should be common to all models as general regulators that are both attributable to reality and necessary to the model. Originating from a mixture of generalized observations and deductions, these principles become general and necessary within the model (in the sense that their negation would lead to contradictions). Even in reality, they represent a particular form of *necessitation** that may be expressed as *that of which negation is materially impossible*. This does not mean that this form of necessity is drawn from reality only—its constitution requires the deductions of a subject—but only that there should be a certain degree of isomorphism (which is, naturally, approximate only, as these principles get

---

*Meaning a process leading to necessity.

6

modified in the course of their history) between the kind of necessity that is inherent in the construction of models and that which the subject has to assume as being necessary in reality.

The interest of the present research, which involves a situation where one or several drops of water are released into a bowl that is three-quarters full, lies in the fact that it permits the distinction of multiple levels of necessity. These levels can be determined from models that are constructed at successive age levels (beginning at 3 years!) and that tend to fall into categories of what may be described as principles of conservation in a wide sense. They begin with the identity of a single drop of water that is considered not to mix with the rest of the water up to the conservation of the additions in the case of a correct, additive solution including a computation showing why the rising of the water level remains invisible.* In short, this very simple example will serve us to show the complexity at each level of the necessity inherent in physical models and in the wealth of imagined deductions when observed facts contradict expectations, when new models must be formulated to reconcile unexpected facts with the general principles of intelligibility.

The method involves four types of questions. In question 1, we present a thin pipette with a bulb located above the bowl of water. Then we release one drop, but a small cover prevents perception of the fall of the water level in the pipette. The passage of the drop from the pipette into the bowl is, however, visible. We ask the child to mark the initial water level in the bowl and the change, if this is predicted. In question 2, the cover is removed and the child is asked to mark the initial water level on the pipette. Subjects expect to be able to perceive eventually a rise in water level in the bowl. But they cannot perceive it, and we ask them to explain this fact. In question 3, the pipette is replaced by a syringe in direct contact with the water in the bowl so that only the evacuation of the syringe suggests an increase in the quantity of water in the bowl. In question 4, the bowl is filled to the brim and the problem is to explain why n drops do not cause a spill, whereas $n+1$ drops do.

Level IA

The models used at this initial level are dominated by a dichotomy that is in part justified but that, if it persists, introduces complications. These arise from the opposition between the drops as individual entities, which can be seen when it rains (and which one can follow with one's eyes as they roll down on the windowpane), and water as a continuous quantity. This dichotomy is real enough in the physical world because each drop is surrounded by a thin membrane, an

---

*The conservation of a quantity of water with a change in appearance (acquired at 7 years) is not treated here.

analog of which is created on the surface of the water in the bowl by the surface tension. But clearly this dichotomy is valid only for brief moments. Subjects at level IA, however, even though they know that the separate drops contain water,* claim that they do not mix with the mass of water in the bowl but preserve their individuality therein because they contain other things besides water: their apparently intentional mobility endows them with properties characteristic of living things such as self-conservation (previous research has shown that the child's animistic thinking is particularly enduring in the case of drops of water as opposed to other objects that can be manipulated).† As a result, we continually find ambiguities in the relations established between water levels in the bowl and the judged quantity of the water, depending on whether subjects include the drops in it or not (if they "don't go into the water"—that is, do not mix with it, as And says).

And (3;5) in question 1 predicts that there will be *more water*, with a substantial rise in water level. When she sees that it has not changed, she concludes: *It is because the drop sank down* [to the bottom] and therefore no longer acted upon the surface level. As to the amount of water, note the answer that she gives to the following question: "If we put the water back into the glass, will there be more water?" *Yes.* "And if it is drops of water?" *No.* She completes this explanation in question 3 (with the syringe) as follows: "The water rose?" *No, because the drops don't go in the water. It didn't go up because the drop* [located at the bottom] *did not want to.* In question 2, And specifies that the first drop released *will go down farther than that* [pointing to the bottom] and that the second fell *into the water and then it was down there* [at the bottom] *because it saw the other drop.* Note that in spite of appearances, there is no contradiction between "they don't go into the water," meaning that they do not mix with it, and "being in there," meaning to be localized within the bowl. There are even better ways to explain the apparent invariance of the water level: the drop, once released, can become a "bubble," and so it "flew" into another bowl used as a comparison vessel. In question 2, when another drop is released, one of those at the bottom *moved up because it tried to get the other drop; she caught it, but after, they let go* [of each other] *and go into the pipe*—i.e., return into the pipette! In question 4 (filled to the top), the drop will *make it lower* [by hitting the surface conceived as a cover] *and after that it will go up again because when it gets lower it should* [!] *go up again* [elasticity?] and the drops all together (*caught up*) return to the pipette.

Nad (3;8) likewise predicts *more water* and explains similarly the apparent

---

*Some subjects believe that they are partly made of air and can "fly."

---

†With M. Bovet. See J. Piaget et al., "Epistémologie et psychologie de l'identité," *Etudes d'épistémologie génétique*, vol. 24 (Paris: Presses Universitaires de France, 1968).

absence of a rise in water level by the fact that the drops gather at the bottom *there, down there*. But if they rise back up *after they have taken a rest*, they will pile up on the surface [cover], and *it will be higher and higher*, etc. When this anticipated result is not confirmed, Nad proposes simply to *put another mark* [on the wall of the bowl] *so it will get higher*. Having tried this: *I thought they would rise up to see the difference* [in the marks] *on the glass."*

Mic (4;7): The drop *goes into the water*, which *will get deeper here* [at the lowest level]. "Where does the drop go?" *To the bottom*. "Will it stay there?" *It will float toward the top*, hence a *higher* level. But the quantity of water remains the same: *The same amount to drink*; when more drops are added, there will even be *less to drink* because they sink to the bottom. "How can we get more to drink?" *Not let more bubbles go down* [syringe]. "With all that water we put in, do you think there is more water now?" *No, it is always the same*. This pseudoconservation is justified by a beautiful deductive pseudonecessity: *The first drop did not make the water rise, so the second one won't do it either: it will go where the first one went, and that's where it is going to stay.*

Car (4;3) does not provide us with any additional information, except that she considers that the drop can be anywhere in the water and that one could find it somewhere. Further, she believes that it could "fly" outside of the bowl.

Cri (4;8) prefigures level IB by considering the water in the bowl as an active entity: the drop will make the water rise because if *that thing* [the pipette] *makes it go down, the water makes it rise again*. We cannot see it because *the water hides it*, but *it is moving up again*. In question 2, without the cover, Cri attains commutability: *There* [1 cm above the water level in the bowl] corresponds to *there* [1 cm beneath the initial level in the pipette]. As in question 3 [syringe]; *There is water that goes down and afterward it is there . . . but not right away: it is going up really slowly*. Still, each drop conserves its individuality: it does not mingle with the water, *because it is round* and it circulates like a discrete object within the liquid.

These subjects at level IA begin with a genuine necessity, which goes back even to the sensorimotor stage: if one adds something to a quantity, one obtains an increase. But this increase or addition has an additive sense only if the added elements are homogeneous (for example, piling up blocks, which even a baby can see) and if the augmented whole is of the same kind as the initial one; in other words, only if the initial and the final quantities are comparable in kind. The peculiarity at level IA resides in the heterogeneity of the discontinuous drops with respect to the continuous water in the bowl receiving them. Where, then, is the increase? Is it the water as such? But it is not modified by the drops. Is it the level, which should rise with each addition? But this one cannot perceive, and one does not know whether the level (which remains the same) is that of the water without the drops (which are hidden at the bottom) or the water plus the drops when these rise back up to the surface. None of these quantification questions is, thus, free of serious ambiguities: when subjects initially predict "more water," this only means "more of something in the bowl." After verification, subjects do not attribute any change to the quantity of water as such, as a result of the drops added (And, Mic, and others, except for the intermediate case of Cri). The water level only depends on the position of the drops, at the bottom or at the surface, even to the point where they might rise to "see the difference" in the position of the mark (Nad)! The only constancy is the conservation of the drop with its surprising powers of self-preservation (identity) within and outside of the bowl and that of the displacements comparable to those of an immutable solid.

Level IB

We class at level IB all those subjects who consider that the drops, being themselves water, mix with the water in the bowl and who, at least in question 2 (without the cover), mention commutability (=what is taken away at the beginning gets added to the result) to explain quantitative increases. These subjects thus believe that there is an increase in the quantity of water. Some of the subjects remain at level IA for question 1 and only progress to level IB for question 2.

Sam (3;10), despite her young age, is already intermediate between levels IA and IB. When the first drop falls, she says: *You put a little water into the glass.* "Can you see it? . . . There [the water mark], has it changed?" *That remains the same*, [but] *that* [the drop falling into the bowl] *has to go there* [into the water]. But despite this good start (with explicit commutability), Sam claims first that the water in the bowl *remains the same*. However, comparing two glasses *A* and *B*, into which one releases one and two drops, respectively, she concludes that *there* [*B*], *there is more*. In question 2, she deduces right away that after the release of the drop, *there* [the pipette] *will be less and there* [the bowl] *will be more water.*

Yvo (4;7) predicts immediately that the drop will mix with the water. "Where?" *There* [a little underneath the surface]. "Why not before? You can find it again?" *No, it gets mixed.* The first drop: "More to drink or the same?" *The same.* "And with a second drop?" *That will fill it up.* He is surprised at the negative result. However, in question II (that is, without the cover), he immediately states that there is more water in the glass as soon as the first drop falls from the pipette, where he can see the drop in water level.

Yan (5;8) predicts a rise in water level for one drop; then after inspection he concludes that *this way there isn't enough*, but still it makes more to drink. We continue with a second drop, and again he predicts a rise in water level, but a very small one. After the trial: "I can't see any difference." *I can't either* [but] *if you drop three that will go up to there.* The drop *was there* [at the surface] *and then gluck gluck* [got mixed in]! *The water* [of the drops] *goes down, flops into the water and then it makes a ball and* [afterward] *it makes a bunch*. Still, he now changes his mind about quantity: "If we drop one, does it make more to drink?" *No, it's still up to the same mark*. But in question 2 (without the cover), he specifies: *There* [in the pipette] *it is gone down, there is the water that falls* [makes a drop] *and in there* [the pipette] *one can see it, but in there* [the bowl] *you can't see it*. Thus we see implicit commutability.

Tom (5;4) displays the same reasoning in question 3 but is visibly surprised that the water level does not go up: *But I made the water squirt out* [from the syringe].

Lio (6;2), despite his age, remains at level IA for question 1: With one drop *it is the same height: always up to the mark*. "What to do?" *The water cannot rise from the drops, only from the faucet. . . . Drops, that's not the same*. "One drop does not make more water?" *That makes only a little water*. "But more?" *No, that doesn't make more: it makes a little drop, that's all*! However, in question 2, he immediately (without waiting for the outcome) predicts: *In the bowl it goes up, in the pipe it goes down*. This belief in commutability is so strong that Lio, disappointed by the first drop, declares with the second drop: *It starts to rise*, and with the third, *It rises*, when, in fact, nothing is perceptible. We remind him of his denials in question 1: *In the other one, it also went up*. Since we remain skeptical, he attenuates: *It isn't risen yet, it is going to rise*.

Lor (6;2), in question 1, predicts: *If you add something, it's going to rise*, indicating the level. Then he observes: *It stayed there*. "But isn't there more water?" *The same amount. Normally it should go up, but it stayed there*. "Why?" *Because you have added a really small drop*. "What about a big one?" *Then there would be more to drink*. In question 2 (without the cover): *Oh, yes, one can see it, because you put the mark there* [on the pipette], *one can see it* [the place where it starts]. "And in the bowl?" *It has already mixed with the water*. "So it makes more?" *A very small amount*. "Necessarily?" *No, but if you add a very big drop, then necessarily there would be more water*. We lower the pipette down to the water level. "Now, if I press?" *Into the container*. "Necessarily? Does one know?" *No*. "But if there is one drop less here [in the pipette], does that not make one drop more there?" *Yes, because one could see that you have added a drop*. "And if one does not see [the difference in water level in the pipette]?" *There is no way to know except by seeing*.

These last statements show the limitations of necessities as conceived at level IB when opposed to the necessary deductions found at level IIA. Still, there is considerable progress when compared with level IA. In recognizing that the drops mix with the water and by treating them as water, the subjects give a new meaning to the question concerning the total sum: the two addenda become homogeneous – the water in the bowl plus the added drops – and there is conservation in the quantitative union of the two entities, conceived now as simple addition. The problem is then to understand why the water level in the bowl does not seem to change since, if (as Lor predicts) there will be more water, then normally the water level should rise, which is not the case. Thus, subjects can be seen, in question 1, to oscillate between two solutions that may be contradictory from one moment to another: either there is not any more water because the drop was too small (but no longer, as at level IA, because they hide at the bottom), or there is more water but one cannot see it. The first of these two solutions (the same amount of water in spite of the addition of a drop) is paradoxically related to the absence of operational conservation in these subjects. As much as an object's quantity changes when its form varies, in the same way it conserves its quantity when an addition is too small to affect its form. The second solution is the result of a beginning understanding of commutability, which becomes general and explicit in question 2. As soon as the water level falls in the pipette, when a drop leaves it, there must be an addition in the bowl corresponding to the subtraction in the pipette. These two models are thus subordinated to a more or less generalized principle of conservation: at level IA, this is limited to the drop as a unit, whereas at level IB it gets extended to the two addenda, which makes it possible to perform an addition; however, the restriction remains that there must be a perceivable change in form (the first solution), which is lifted in the second solution with the extension to all those cases where commutability can be invoked. Nevertheless, even in these cases there remains the need to see the departure and the arrival of the drop before one can conclude that there is necessarily more water. Thus, there is only a beginning, not yet generality, of deductive necessity. The latter will be found at level IIA.

Level IIA

At level IIA, subjects affirm an increase in quantity as soon as one drop is added, even though there is no perceptible change in water level:

Cal (6;3) predicts that the drop *sinks down deep, and then it displaces the water and the water rises.* "One can see the drop?" *No, it gets compressed and becomes like the rest of the water. . . . It is part of the water.* (Question 1, one drop). *One does not see anything.* "Why?" *Because the water is wet, it rises slowly.* In question 2: *The water will rise.* "Necessarily?" *Yes, one can see it because one can see the drop come down.*

Gab (6;2): *The water will go up.* One drop is added. *Nothing happened* [laughs]. "But is there more water or not?" *A tiny little bit more, because we saw it drip into the water.* Question 2: Similar reactions but also: *One doesn't see it, because the bowl is bigger* [than the pipette].

San (7;5), in question 1: *The drop floated, then it sank and the water rose a little.* "Are you sure?" *Yes.* "Could it have been different?" *No, it is like that—it has to go.* Question 3: *There is more water, but one can't see much of it, enough to see it in the bowl.*

Joa (7;7), after one drop: "Is there more water?" *Just a tiny bit more, because we've added a tiny drop.* "How can one be sure?" *One knows because something was added.* Question 2: *There* [in the pipette], *there is less water, and there* [in the bowl] *there is more.* Question 3: *A tiny bit more in the bowl, but we can't see it, because the bowl is large.*

Ali (7;5) predicts spontaneously that *there will be a bit more water* [but] *we won't be able to see it.* The first reason given (after one, two, three, and four drops) is that *we have to wait until there are at least five drops* for the water to rise perceptibly; then, a second explanation: *A single drop is not enough* to be seen, but it *will go up. They have to, there is no other way.*

Mar (8;0), after the first drop: *That's not great* [nothing can be seen], *but still it rose.* "Inevitably?" *Yes.*

Syl (8;2): *It does rise a bit. I can't see it, but I know that it becomes more.*

Mir (8;8): *There will be more to drink. But it is so little that you can't see it.* In question 2: *You took some out* [in the pipette] *and I could see the difference* [true], *but I did not see the difference in the glass. . . . But* [still] *there will be more.*

Sca (8;1) *One cannot see it, but one knows it.*

Cat (8;4) has similar reactions in question 1. Question 2: "Why does one not see anything here [in the bowl]?" *Because in the glass, it is larger, and there* [in the pipette] *it is thin.*

Pat (9;0): *It dropped down but you won't see it in the bowl: it is much bigger compared with the pipe.*

Necessity as conceived at this level (IIA) is clearly already deductive in question 1 – that is, there is no need to observe the drop in water level in the pipette. This deductive character manifests itself in explicit verbal form: one cannot see, but "one knows" (Syl and Sca), there is "necessarily" more water (Cal, Mar, etc.), "it is like that" (San), the drops "have to [make the water rise], there is no other way" (Ali). These deductions consist in spatial and causal co-necessary compositions, integrating the conservation of the drop (level IA) with the invariance of its liquid nature when mixed with the rest of the water (level IB) and adding to this the interactions with the water already present in the bowl: the drop "sinks down deep. . . . [After that] it gets compressed and becomes like the rest of the water" (Cal). This includes, since water is "added," a necessary rise in water level, even if it cannot be seen. A few subjects add a spatial composition explaining why this rise is imperceptible: the bowl is too "large" (Joan and Cat) or "big" (Gab and Pat) compared with the pipe, which is "thin" and where the changes in water level are visible. In general this deductive necessity derives from compositions, of which subjects determine not only the relationships and laws but also the reasons or causes. These are based, already in question 1, on commutability: what is subtracted at the start (pipette) must be added at the goal (the bowl). This explains the rise in water level, which is necessary even though invisible ("not great," as Mar notes, "but still it rose").

We should note that it is possible to distinguish, within level IIA, certain phases according to the way the subjects envision the mixing of the drops with the water in the bowl: (1) the individual drop remains in the water; (2) two drops "catch up with one another"; (3) a small bundle of drops; (4) a big bundle; and (5) a homogeneous mixture, where individual drops disappear. Subjects' drawings show these phases. One of them first draws a drop falling from the pipette just above the water level, then crosses out this drawing to make another where the lower end of the pipette makes contact with the water surface. This renders the mix more "necessary."

Levels IIB and III

The same kinds of responses are given at the usual age for level IIB (9–10 years of age), but there is also a search for ways to prove the rise in water level even though it is invisible.

Gov (8;0): Can one see the *more water* (which he asserts without hesitating)? *No. One has to be more precise: something with centimeters on it in the water, and then one could look: the water does not even change by a fourth of a millimeter.*

Cer (8;11): *One should weigh it.*

Ric (9;6): *One cannot see it,* but with a projection from the water level increasing the differences (he shows ⟨) *one could see it on the wall.*

Jol (10;3): To see the change in water level *one would need special lenses.*

Lex (10;0): *One cannot see it with the naked eye,* [but] *with a microscope.*

Did (11;0): *One would have to take the water out of the bowl and measure it.*

These responses can easily be interpreted as attempts to show what one should do to verify objectively the rise in water level, which cannot be perceived with the naked eye but can be deduced with necessity (these subjects begin, of course, by giving the arguments described in IIA). In other words, subjects at level IIB, having constructed the deductive model they judge to be necessary, ask themselves simply how it can be tested. This is, mutatis mutandis, what physicists do.

Subjects at level III take a different direction. They are not interested in how to verify that there is a rise in water level, but rather how one can explain the fact that the change remains invisible. This problem was approached at level IIA by Joa, Gab, Cat, and Pat when they correctly contrasted the size of the bowl with that of the pipette from which the drop falls. This idea is taken up again by the 12- to 13-year-olds, with the following development:

Jos (12;11): *Certainly, there is more water, but when the drop is in the water, it can no longer be seen.* "Why?" *Well! Because the bowl is bigger and the pipe is smaller.* She then draws a drop falling onto the surface in the bowl and spreading over the surface for a distance of about two-thirds of the diameter. Specifying that the latter measures about 35 cm and that of the syringe about 3 cm, she considers it possible that these measures will tell about *the way the drop spreads* [again on the surface]. In short, the idea is that one could calculate the minimal height corresponding to the spread of the drop over the surface. She specifies further that *this depends on the bowl: if it is small, one would be able to see some change.*

Myl (13;4) starts with the same model but specifies that *it takes a calculation because the drop spreads in width. It did not rise, and what was in the tube was not the same quantity in width. One could measure the water in there* [the pipette] *according to the width and the water there* [the bowl] *by the diameter.* She demonstrates this with three drawings. "Do you need three?" *Yes, even more than three, if one really wants to know what is going on, otherwise one cannot see the action.* Then Myl adds a hypothesis: *When the drop gets in there* [the water], *that takes air out. When it drops it sinks in, making a small hollow, and the drop spreads out over that hollow.* In that case, *when you inject, that makes some air escape . . . Well, that makes more liquid:* [in] *the glass you fill with drops, there is more water and less air.* This explains the fact that the change in water level is not visible.

Ben (13;3) offers the same two-way model (water level and air), but in addition sums up: *The drop settles down on top. It spreads over the whole dimension there* [surface]. *Not necessarily in a layer, but it rises, it depends on the surface. One can calculate this.* It follows from this that the drop remains small in height, since it spreads over a large surface. But still *there is no change, because there is air in there and the drop takes the place of the air.*

These subjects thus add to the model established at level IIA (which showed that there is necessarily an increase in the amount of water) explanatory models designed to show why this increase is imperceptible. The first interesting point is that Myl is aware of constructing a model. "One cannot see the action," she says, and "if one really wants to know what is going on," one needs a deductive construction illustrated by drawings — or what other subjects call a computation. On this higher level there thus appear new kinds of necessities that result not simply from a reading of facts, as at level IIA (a drop was passed form the pipette to the bowl, therefore the latter must necessarily contain more water). Rather, it results from hypothetical events that are capable of explaining why the increase is imperceptible: (1) the drop spreads over the surface so that, necessarily, it becomes minimal in height; (2) the water contains air and the drop "takes its place" (Ben), so necessarily there is little variation in height.

Whether these hypotheses are true or false is of less interest than the fact that the conclusions subjects draw from them are deductively necessary, but of a kind of necessity that is both more hypothetical and more inferential than at level IIA. This characterizes a new level of necessity.

Conclusions

To begin with the general problem we raised in the beginning of this chapter, we shall first discuss the relative contributions of the subject and the object in what appears to be the most constrained necessity recognized by all subjects in their initial predictions: the fact that the addition of a certain quantity of a substance no matter how small (a drop), to another quantity of the same substance (the contents of the bowl) results in a quantitative increase of the latter substance. At first sight, there seems to be here the prototype of a "real necessity" that is inherent in objects, which we have found questionable in the discussion at the beginning of this chapter. But what exactly does reality, taken as the universe of observables, tell us with respect to this question? Certainly, if there is addition, there is always quantitative increase. But this is either a simple tautology—to add=to increase, which has necessity only in the subject's language—or else it is a general fact but one that has no necessity so long as certain terms remain unspecified: the exact nature of the addenda, what exactly summation means, and what precisely their quantitative character consists in. In particular, we do not know whether the addenda or the sums change in the course of the successive additions. For instance, Ben (level III) proposes that the drop that enters expels air, which means that the addition of the first term (the drop) to the second (the bowl) expels an equivalent portion of air so that the increase is compensated for by an equivalent decrease. This is not in contradiction with increase, but it shows that, to proceed from a statement of generality (generalization) to that of a necessity, one must construct models that specify precisely how to interpret observables and what meaning should be given to the quantitative concepts to be used.

Our data tell us that there are at least four different types of models. All of them incorporate, more or less successfully, the notion that an addition brings about a quantitative increase; that is, they are based on a common principle that could be labeled *conserving additivity*. This principle has general utility because it also applies to logico-mathematical operations such as $2+1=3$ or $A+A'=B$ (where $B>A$ and $B>A'$, where only A and A' intervene and nothing is lost from the union class).

The level IA model applies this principle only to the drops themselves, to which the subjects attribute an imaginary conservation beyond observability: the drops are held to conserve their identity all the way to the inside of the bowl, in the air (in the form of bubbles), and even in the pipette when they wait to return to it. This conservation permits additivity, since one drop can "catch up to" another (And), separate from it, or "pile up" on the surface, which is seen as a kind of cover (Nad). When Sam (level IB) regresses momentarily to level IA, she claims that even though the drops do not raise the water level in the bowls, there is "more" in a bowl where two drops were added compared with another where only one drop was added. But sometimes the absence of any relationship between the drops and the water in the bowl may go as far as is seen in Mic, who affirms that since "the first drop did not make the level rise, so the second one won't do it either." Briefly, the conserving additivity characteristic of level IB only concerns the drops, which do not enter into the sum as addenda of the same kind as the water in the bowl. As for the quantity of water, one observes oscillation between the supposition that it does not change, because the drops are "something different" — but this amounts to a pseudoconservation — and the hypothesis (usually emitted in making predictions) that it increases under the impact of the drops. The latter cannot be considered as true addition.

The model used at level IB shows progress in the use of the principle of conserving additivity, since the drops are now seen as "mixing" with the water so that we can speak of additivity, the addenda being homogeneous so that they can each be subject to quantitative conservation both during and after their summation. At this intermediate level, in question 1 (with the cover), it is not enough for the subjects to see the drop fall into the bowl and mix with the water: they do not assert addition, since the water level has not changed. This explains the constant vacillation in subjects' assessment of the final result. They see that something is added but with no quantitative increase, the drop being too small. In spite of the union of the addenda and their homogeneity, subjects still have problems with the final result (the sum). In contrast, in question 2, things become clearer because subjects can see the drop in water level in the pipette as soon as the drop leaves it. Now the transfer of the add drop leads subjects to see that necessarily there is addition and hence an increase in water level in the bowl, even if it remains invisible. Thus, they begin to see the commutability of the addenda (less water in the pipette and therefore more water in the bowl, as noted by Sam); this commutability then leads to the conserving additivity for the entire system (water and drops) rather than only for the drops. The special interest of this model from level IB is that, in the absence of a visible change in water level, additivity (more water because of the drop) does not appear as necessary to the subjects unless they can see the drop in water level in the pipette, which to them should bring about an equivalent (albeit invisible) rise in the bowl: $-g$ (pipette) $= +g$ (bowl).

The next model (level IIA) extends this conserving additivity to question 1 — that is, without the perceptual support afforded by the direct comparison of levels. Thus, necessity is now largely independent of observables and clearly demonstrates the deductive and endogenous nature of the principle (X conserved) $+ (Y$ conserved) $= (X + Y) > X$. Level IIB retains the same model, only adding the idea of possible experimental controls if one had the appropriate measuring tools. However, at level III a fourth type of model appears, which projects explanations for the fact that the changes in water level remain invisible: computation of the relationship between water level and the spread of the drop on the surface or the hypothesis of air expulsion compensated for by the water of the drop.

Throughout this developmental sequence, the growth of necessity is apparently related to models constructed by the subject, where observables naturally serve as indispensable aids to deductions but only as interpreted exogenous data. Necessity—unreducible to generality—never constitutes an observable among others. With the exception of the model at level IA and its pseudonecessity of the individualized drops, which gets replaced at the next level by the necessity of the conservation of the water they contain, each model is integrated in the next one. This continual integration of the lower within the higher-level model constitutes, as we shall repeatedly show in the following chapters, the principal characteristic or even the origin of a single process, which is the growth of necessities.

But if it is the case that necessity is endogenous in character and that reality in itself remains only necessitated, how can one account for the fact that the models subjects attribute to objects succeed so well that they become necessitating? In other words, what explains the isomorphism relating the objects that are subjected to subjects' treatment and the subjects reconstructing them deductively? The answer is that the subject—who is simultaneously object, as an organism and by the material actions she performs with the objects—derives from them her "operations"; these operations she coordinates according to certain general principles of composition, which are common to all her models and have for effect a synthesis of transformations and conservations to form closed systems. These principles, of which we just analyzed an example with the case of conserving additivity, constitute the conditions for all intelligibility. Therefore they are applicable to all objects, physical as well as conceptual or mental ones, which really amounts to support for the claim that reality is intelligible. Finally, if one wishes to raise the question as to the reason of this intelligibility, the answer can only be that the subject is fundamentally nothing but an active object among other objects, but whose activity is self-regulated and tends to encompass retroactively all other objects by virtue of her biologically grounded capacity of cognitive assimilation.

2

Necessity and Impossibility in Compositions of Rotations

with A. Blanchet and D. de Capona

In our search for the reasons for the probable isomorphisms between the necessities constructed by the subject with her models of reality and whatever in reality can be posited as necessary (since our models are successful to some degree), without being directly accessible to our perception, chapter 1 has provided a first example of mediators in the form of principles common to logico-mathematical systems and to physical models — such as the principle of conservation. But there exists an even more general mediator, which is space. In fact, we have a geometry of the subject as well as a space of objects, and, in spite of their internal differences (which are considerable), there never has been a contradiction between the two, except for a virtual infinity of space in the mind of the subject that evidently goes beyond the limits of reality.

Where elementary rotations are concerned, we can distinguish three forms with respect to the subject-object relation. First, the sensorimotor level already displays rotations due to actions the subjects exert upon themselves: turning around in a circle, turning their hands or their head. Second, almost as early, subjects can rotate objects to explore their different sides. Third, objects can also rotate independently of a subject, such as a rock rolling down a slope. Many more circular rotations are observable in the real world. What these three types of rotation have in common is that they all follow the same structural laws — those of cyclical groups. This chapter concerns not the comprehension of these laws, but the necessity inherent in the pathways of a single element (a chip) resulting from three kinds of rotation (one complete turn) or semirotations (half a turn) performed by the support to which it is attached. These notions may be carried out one at a time or in combinations. The problem to be analyzed is the subjects' activity with the apparatus. We wish to determine which procedures are used, from simple readings of facts all the way to deductive predictions, to arrive at the judgments of necessity and impossibility that are characteristic of different levels of development. This is a very simple situation where the geometry of objects and that of the subject can be seen together. It may be particularly informative with respect to the general question concerning the origin and mechanism of the growth of necessity.

The material consists of two square frames that rotate about an axis, one rotating about a horizontal axis (*H*) and the other, located inside the first, about a vertical axis (*V*). The whole arrangement rests upon a third square frame, which rotates about its center (*R*). If one places a chip anyplace on the inner

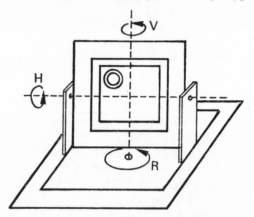

frame, one can make it reappear in its initial position either by rotating any one of the three frames by one complete turn or by combining a semirotation *V* with another semirotation *R*, since the two frames rotate about the same axis. It is also possible to make the chip occupy a position on the same surface, symmetrical with respect to the intersection of the *V* and *H* axes, by combining two semirotations *H* and *V* (or *R*). The direction and the sequence of the two rotations are not important. It is, however, impossible to have the chip occupy other symmetrical positions with respect to the different axes without shifting to the other side by means of simple semirotations.

A chip is attached to one of the upper corners of the inner frame. The procedure consists in posing the series of problems just described to get the subject to understand the combinations, which bring to the fore implicit and explicit necessities. In addition, we analyze the results obtained after changing the initial position of the chip in the course of the experiment, after adding other chips, or when subjects are asked to represent graphically the different, successive positions of the chip.

Level IA

At 5 to 6 years of age, subjects typically show a total absence of combinations, and simple rotations are not always understood as being composed of two semirotations of which the second leads back to the point of origin and constitutes an inversion of the first. On the other hand, subjects naturally achieve a few successful performances by simple trial and error. These can even be generalized to further instances, but without any comprehension of necessities:*

Ena (5;0): "Can you make it move?" He exerts a weak action on *H*. "Can it move more?" *No.* "Try." (One-half *R*.) Ena then discovers *V* and *R*, so we attach the chip to *1*: "We can move it and get the chip to return to the same place? . . . Try." He does *V* and its inverse. "If one turns it [two *V*=one complete turn of 360 degrees], does it return to the same place?" *No.* "Can one make it change places?" *No.* "Try." (*V*.) "Where is it?" *On the other side* [in back]. "Can you make it come back?" He turns in the opposite direction. "And by turning something else?" He repeats *V* in both directions. "And if one does this [*H*], one can make it come back to the same place [the initial position]?" He does the inverse. "And from there, one can make it move there[the diagonal]?" *Yes* [he does *V* in both directions]. "Where is it now?" *On the other side* [in back]. "And if one does this [*H*], how can we make it move where my finger is [*4*]?" He performs only one *H* and positions it in "back" but to the right. We show him how to combine *V*×*H*, but his imitation consists of two *H* only.

Mag (5;6), much more active, explores *R*, *V*, ad *H*, then concludes that to make the chip return to the same place *1* it takes many *H*. "And if you turn something else?" She tries with a three-quarter *R*. *No.* She tries again with many *H*. "Sometimes one needs to turn a lot? And if you turn something, one can make it go there[4]? . . . Where is it?" *Still there in the same place.* "Does it sometimes change sides?" *No. It's there, in back.* "I think one can make it go there. Try." *Let's try to turn it a bit faster* [many *H*]. "If you go fast, it goes there?" *Let's see* [many *H* and one *V* by accident]. *Let's try to do it like a turnstile.* She thus seems to understand that *V* is necessary, but starts again with *H* alone: *We'll turn fast. That will bring it back to its place.* She then happens to turn, in random fashion, *H* and *R* simultaneously, but only concludes: *I turned like that* [*R* alone] *and it's gone there.* For the impossible position *2* (upper right): *If one turns* H *it's in back and if one turns* H *once again, it's the same. So I don't know how to do it.* But for the lower left, also impossible, she continues with the *H*.

Jea (5;11) begins by knocking the frame instead of turning it slowly (cf. with the speed in Mag's case). For the diagonal, he adds turns *H*×*H*×*V*×*H*; but the only conclusion he comes to is: *When you turn several times like that* H, *sometimes it ends up on the bottom* [in front], *sometimes on top.* He deduces from

---

*For brevity, we shall adopt the following notation: *V* for a semirotation (180 degrees), one-half *V* for a quarter rotation, etc. We shall denote as *1* the initial location of the chip in the upper left; *2* the impossible position (in front) in the upper right, but "2 in back" when it is correct; *3* the position in the lower left (impossible in front); and *4* the position in the lower right (also called diagonal).

this, and demonstrates with a drawing, that the chip can end up in the two impossible positions, 2 and 3; he fails to show the only possible position (4); he is right in expressing doubts about the possibility of rotating the chip to a central position but keeps trying nevertheless by performing many uncoordinated rotations. With several chips fastened to the square, he tries many times to see whether it is possible that some chips change their locations while others remain in the same positions. With four chips he expects to find only two horizontal permutations. Confronted with the results, he exclaims: *I don't know how that could change. There is no invisible hand.*

Sar (5;6) appears to understand quickly that a turn R makes the chip appear to the right (2) in back and that another turn V can bring it back to its point of departure. But then she indicates the same position (2) in back as the result of a turn H, likewise with a possible return by means of V. In other words, she does not distinguish between the directions H, V, and R, even though she understands that by continuing each turn one obtains the initial position: *You have to turn once more* [another half turn] *and it comes back.* After she had obtained, by chance, position 4, we ask what to do "to get there." *We turned that [V] and it came back to there* [on the right]. "What else?" *That [R]. We turned that [R] and that one [V].* But 4 can only be obtained by $V \times H$ or $H \times R$. She adds: *You have to do that [R]: it is down,* as if this would make the chip come down. In the following (not comprehending why two positions are impossible), Sar adds H to V and sees the change from 1 to 4: "And to make it come back? Two $V \times$ inverse of $V \times H$, then $V \times H$, then two $V \times H \times$ two R and $H \times H \times V \times H$ (success). "If its house is here [2], where will it go?" *There [4,* an impossible position in this case]. "I, for my part, believe it is there [3]." She repeats $V \times H$ six times before being convinced. "What if we put up two chips, A in position 1 and B in position 2?" *They will go there [A on 3 below 1 and B on 4 below 2].* "Which one will go there [2]?" *Ah, the A here [4] and B there [2]:* in other words, she generalizes the familiar paths $1 \rightarrow 4$ and $2 \rightarrow 3$.

The observed phenomena are of interest with regard to the relation between the geometry of objects (the rotations of the square) and that of the actions appropriate to select, direct, and coordinate these rotations. From an empiricist viewpoint, one might have predicted that the subjects at this initial level, even though or perhaps because they are as yet incapable of making predictions, would simply register the unexpected observations but in a sufficiently objective way to be able to generalize and to combine them to achieve the various goals. Yet, the truth of the matter is not at all like that. The two principal characteristics of these reactions are, on the one hand, the complete absence of combinations and, on the other, the main reason for this absence—the failure to distinguish adequately between the two kinds of rotation, one of which takes place on the vertical (H), the other two on the horizontal plane (V and R remain identical as long as the square with the chip remains vertical; R becomes equivalent to $V \times H$

if the square is placed horizontally, which has not been done in interviewing the youngest subjects). The observables are thus usable only if they are "comprehended" by means of a necessitating action, which depends on the subject's ability to coordinate the various acitons. But this ability only develops later, since it has for prerequisites the joint effects of two interrelated processes: one internalizing one—that is, the growth of consciousness and reflecting abstractions; the other an externalizing one that increases objectivity in terms of better differentiation and control of results as a function of progress in internal organization.

At level IA, the interaction between the geometry of subjects' actions and that which subjects discover in objects is to some extent negative or neutral: the deficiencies in one interfere with the development of the other. Only later does this interaction become positive so that there develops a mutual facilitation between the two. The absence of an understanding of combinations is clearly evident in subjects like Ena, who not only has no idea of a possible link between two different rotations but who does not even understand the demonstration we give her of combining $V \times H$, which she imitates by doing H alone. Similarly, Mag, after having produced accidentally an association between H and R, is aware only of having turned R "and it's gone there," without, of course, understanding how. Sar after a similar success only retains her action on V in her explanations; however, later on she succeeds in adding H to V but falters a long time to obtain the return.

The reason for this absence of compositions provides the key to an understanding of the reactions characteristic of this level with reference to the two complementary difficulties just discussed—i.e., the capacity to come to a conscious awareness and thus to self-regulate one's actions and the incomplete analysis of the observables. As we have seen, subjects do not differentiate the three kinds of rotation with respect to the directions they give to them. Thus, Mag seeks to obtain the intended direction by repeating the H rotation many times and by speeding them up. Later, when she realizes the need for a lateral motion, she correctly remarks that it would take a rotation "like a turnstile," or on a horizontal plane. This understanding, however, does not prevent her from using, once again, the rotation H, the only one that operates in the vertical plane, and, seeing that this does not work, from suggesting, "We'll turn fast. That will bring it back to its place." Jea suggests that, when using H, "sometimes it ends up on the bottom [in front], sometimes on top." Sar uses R because "it is down [below]," believing that this will make the chip go down. Similarly, with two chips, she thinks at first that they will follow a parallel course. Only later does she generalize what she has seen—that is, the change in location from $1 \rightarrow 4$ and from $2 \rightarrow 3$.

There remains the interesting problem of simple rotations and their return to the point of departure. A complete turn of two V, two H, or two R (i.e., 360 degrees, since *V, H,* and *R* denote a 180 degree rotation) is not yet understood as being composed of two semirotations. Thus, Ena refuses to believe that the complete turn would reinstate the initial position. Even when Mag carries out a series of rotations and notes these momentary returns, she is not aware that a single, complete rotation would be sufficient. Only Sar is aware of this fact and thus comes close to level IB reasoning. What all subjects at level IA understand, however, is the return by following the same path in the opposite direction, which cancels the effect of each half-rotation *V, H,* or *R*. We shall express this type of inversion as $(X \rightarrow Y) + (X \leftarrow Y) =)$. It constitutes the first and only form of local necessity that is accessible to level IA thinking.

Except for the elementary form of inversion just discussed, one can say that at level IA everything seems possible but nothing appears necessary because of a lack of comprehension of both the mechanisms involved in the subjects' own actions, which remain unanalyzed as to their spatial characteristics, and of the observable relationships between the moving objects. Nevertheless, there is good correspondence between the geometry of the object and that of the subject in terms of their inadequacies as well as their reciprocal facilitation.

Level IB

Even though the difficulties experienced by subjects at level IB are identical to those at level IA, there is important progress in that subjects comprehend the involution of a complete turn of two *H,* two *V,* or two *R,* which necessarily reinstates the initial position.

Kar (6;5) turns *H, V,* and *R* and concludes: *It turns completely.* We ask her, "How do you turn to make it come back to the same place?", to which she replies immediately: *Two times that way* [*V*]. "Does it work?" *Yes* [tries]. *I turned like that and I've turned once more and it returns there.* But with two chips, one in position *1* and the other in position *4,* she tries and concludes: *To see if it works, I turned there* [*V*] *and then I turned there* [the second *V*], *and they returned to the same place.* "Can you make *1* go to *4*? *No, it is impossible! When one turns, it goes there in back, one doesn't know where.* (She does *H.* "Where is it now?" *There* [she points to the back of *1*], *up there, but to make it return, one can't know where. . . . Oh, no, it is down there* [behind *3*]. "And what about *4*?" *Ah! I know: turn that one* [*V*=correct]. Then, having empirically verified the impossibility of the transfer *1→2,* she cannot figure out the reason, even though she understands that *V*×*R* (which she tries out) results in two rotations in the horizontal plane (where they are identical). The same error for the change *2→4,* where she proposes *H,* but she believes that in that case the chip remains behind *2* or goes behind *4*; she notes that it is behind *4* and rightly concludes that *if one turns* R, *it goes there* [*3*]. With two chips in locations *1* and *2,* she correctly predicts (generalizing from the preceding trials) that their possible paths are

1→4 and *2→3*. But when we add a third one in the middle, she concludes that those paths become impossible *because the green one is there* [in the path]. That is, she forgets, as in the case of *1→2* and *2→4*, that the circular motions impose circular pathways on the chips rather than displacements on a linear plane.

Lau (6;6), in position *1*, rotates the chip *V×V*, *H×H*, and *R×R*. "Can you do 1→4?" She tries *H×V*, then: *No, you can't get it there, but you can there* [*1→2*]. She tries but finds that with *V* or *H*, the chip remains hidden. She adds a rotation, *V×H*. "And to make it return?" (Again, *V×H*.) She then executes a series of 12 rotations, *R*, *V*, and *H*, to try to get *1→3*. She notices that the chip goes in back. This does not prevent her, with two chips in positions *1* and *2* and a third in the center, from thinking that the third chip will come to be between the other two or will descend from its central position to one near the bottom of the square (she tries more than 15 *H*, *V*, and *R* combined to obtain this result). "How do you explain that this one goes from *1* to *4*, when the other one is in the way?" *It goes like that* [demonstrates a curved line in the plane]. For three chips in a row and then five, one in each corner and the fifth in the center, she can only predict translatory and reverse motions.

Val (6;6) immediately carries out *V×V*, *H×H*, and *R×R*. For *1* to *4*, *of course*: H . . . ×V [hesitating]. "Another way?" He does *H×H*, etc., then looking at *R* discovers *H×R*. He tries to do *1* to *2*, in vain, but still believes that the chip could *land in all four corners, because those gadgets turn.*

Three kinds of reactions characterize level IB, of which two seem contradictory. The first is the comprehension of the complete rotation carried out by the center square, whether it turns in a vertical direction by using *H* or in a lateral motion with *V* or *R*. By coordinating two semirotations, subjects inevitably return the chip to its initial position (*1*, *2*, etc.). Subjects thus discover a second necessity, which remains local, however (we shall see why), after the one involving inversion $[(+V)×(-V)=)]$, which was already present at level IA. The second reaction is that, having performed the three kinds of rotation and having distinguished them—a progress that contrasts with the lack of differentiation found at level IA—subjects come up with the idea, when the situation becomes more complex and they fail to obtain the desired result with one rotation (*H* for *1→4* in Kar, *V* or *H* in Lau), to turn two squares at the same time. This leads to success (*V×H*), after trials and errors and without anticipation nor subsequent generalization (except for partial ones; see Kar's experience with two chips). Thus we may say that subjects attempt combinations in empirical ways but as yet give no evidence of planned compositions. Finally, the third type of reaction, which seems consistent with the second and its hesitations but contradictory with the first, is that, even though subjects carry out the rotations of the center square, they believe that the chip attached to it in various positions can move around in translatory and visible fashion on the surface of the square. They believe this, even though their experience shows that the chip tends to pass through on the other side and become invisible. From this experience they should know that such translatory motion is impossible, given the characteristics of the device. The most astonishing reactions are those with respect to the center chip, which subjects see as an obstacle to the path $1 \rightarrow 4$, since they have seen that in going from 1 to 4 the chip passes through 2 on the back side. Still, they seem to believe the chip to be able to take independent rectilinear pathways.

Level IIA

With respect to the motive behind the $V \times H$ compositions, the difference between IB and IIA is not easy to discern because the procedures of level IIA remain largely empirical. However, one can describe this difference in terms of the fact that at level IB subjects resort to a second rotation (V after H only in Kar, etc.) only after first failing with a single rotation, whereas at level IIA subjects very soon understand the necessity of coordinating the two forms, right-left and up-down; yet they still do not anticipate the composition to be chosen and only discover it after having received some cues. On the other hand, the linear pathways of level IB are no longer observed.

Jac (7;5), to obtain $1 \rightarrow 4$, notes spontaneously that with H alone the chip cannot be positioned on the right side: *I have to put it there* [2] *and turn.* She then tries V with R and notes: *It stayed on the same side* [visible], so she combines R and H. "Another way?" *No.* "Without moving R?" ($H \times V$.) "And return to 1?" ($V \times H$.) To get $1 \rightarrow 3$: *I think to make it go there* [3] *I have to put it there* [2, thus ✓]. As for $1 \rightarrow 2$, *I don't know yet.* She tries several times and concludes: *I think it is the same thing as here* [$1 \rightarrow 3$]: *it can't be done.*

Cat (7;0) immediately shows the returns two V, two H, and two R. "What if you turn two squares at once?" *Yes* [tries $H \times V$]. *No.* When we go on to $1 \rightarrow 4$, she proposes $H \times V$, having already seen that two different rotations do not bring about a return. ($H \times R$.) "Is it possible to do $1 \rightarrow 3$?" *Yes* [tries $H \times V$]. *No.* "Can it be done?" *No. The only place to go starting from 2 is 3.* Her drawing of the possible positions starting from 1 marks the visible positions, 1 and 4, with a circle and two invisible ones, 2 and 3, with a cross. "If I put two chips up [1 and 2]?" *The red one can go there* [$1 \rightarrow 4$] *and the blue one there* [$2 \rightarrow 3$]; thus, two diagonals. "And if I put one in the middle?" *It will always stay in the middle.*

Nat (7;0), for $1 \rightarrow 4$: *I don't know how to do it*; then, after some thinking, she tries $H \times R$ and also discovers $V \times R$. Her comment is instructive: *I turned that* [V], *but I don't remember which way and then I turned R and I don't remember which way*; she adds, *I am thinking about the direction*, referring naturally to the different directions to be combined, as well as to the forward ($+$) and the backward ($-$) directions.

Ste (8;11) is explicit in this respect: for $1 \rightarrow 4$, one has to *first lower the square* [including the chip] *and then turn.* His drawing shows the chip moving downward from the visible position *1* to the invisible *3* and from *3* to *4* (visible). But this casual summary is the result of a series of trials and errors wherein he continually tries to come to grips with the directions. The center square being first presented horizontally, Ste takes a look at *the chip and the turn*, then correctly uses a turn *R*. Then with the vertical square and the same question *1→4*, he sees that it is not enough to *turn* but that he has to add a descent using *H*. For *1→2*, he makes a brief attempt, then says: *No, it can't be done; I can make it go there* [to *2* with *V*], *but it remains on the other side* [invisible]. With two chips at *1* and *2*, he immediately predicts *1→4* and *2→3*.

Dan (8;9), for *1→4*, first does not know how to proceed; but when we propose *H*, he adds *V*: *After, I turn that* [*V*]. Having noted the impossible paths, he predicts *2→3*. "How do you know?" *Because I've tried to turn* V *and* H *and it ended up there* [*3*]. Then he recognizes the equivalence of *V×H* and *H×V*. For three chips, *only those in the corners can move*, and the one in the middle *always stays in the same place*.

Iva (8;5), for *1→4*, says, *I don't know*; but then she chooses *H×R*. "How did you know?" *Because if you turn* H, *it's in back, and if you turn* H *again, it comes back to where it was*, therefore she added *V*. When, after many trials, she concludes the impossibility of *1→2* and *1→3*, she explains this by referring to the fact that *the chip always has to come there* [diagonal]: *it's on the same side* [visible]. This leads to immediate correct predictions for the chips in positions *1* and *2*. As for the center chip: *That one always stays there, unless it goes in front or in back*. "The other ones have really changed places?" *No* [laughs], *it's that thing* [the center square] *that moves*.

And (8;0) responds, like Iva, with *perhaps* to the question of moving *1→4*. "How do you think?" He discovers *V×H*: *You turn both of them: it goes down and if you don't turn both at the same time* [= *V* and *H* together], *it stays in the same place* [= the chip returns to *1*]. "What if we put it there [at *2*]?" *That goes there* [to *3*]. "Could it go elsewhere?" *Behind* 1. "And behind *4*?" *No, I don't think so*. "Try anyway." He succeeds.

Xav (8;11), having (like all preceding subjects) successfully accomplished two *R*, etc., tries to turn *H* and *V* *at the same time* but very slowly so that he can watch the process before drawing general conclusions. "Can you do *1→3*?" *I'll try* (V×H, a success). *If it works here* ↘, *it should work there* ✓. For two chips on *1* and *2*, he immediately generalizes. "They have crossed each other?" *They did not cross each other. In fact, the path really goes like this*→ *and like that*↓, *and not directly like that* ↘. His drawings are correct, including symbols to represent the rotations.

In spite of their initial hesitations and constant concern with empirical checks, these subjects show two essential advances with respect to those at level IB. The first is the comprehension of the necessarily circular paths of the chip as determined by the rotations *H, V*, or *R* of the square and the impossibility of linear paths independent of these rotations. This necessity, which is integrated with the two preceding ones (the inversions of level IA and the complete rotations with return of the chip in level IB), is not made explicit by the subjects, for whom it is self-evident. Still, it can be inferred from a great many behaviors. The clearest manifestation can be found in that subjects no longer make reference to translatory motions in the case of two or three chips, as did the level IB subjects. Most importantly they understand that the center chip remains immobile: "It will always stay in the middle," says Cat; "it always stays in the same place," Dan declares; and Iva adds, "unless it goes in front and in back." Xav specifies very clearly that the two other chips "did not cross each other. In fact, the path really goes like this and like that [two rotations], and not directly like that [diagonal translation]." On the other hand, even though the impossible paths are not explained in detail, Cat and others understand (and show this in their drawings) that these paths go from *1* to *2* or *3*, but by passing over to "the other side," as Ste says. Iva makes it clear that a rotation and not a translation is involved: "If you turn *H*, it's in back, and if you turn *H* again, it comes back." And recall her laugh at the question of whether the chip has changed places: "No, it's that thing [the center square] that moves."

The second new acquisition of level IIA (which is undoubtedly related to the preceding one) is that, since a double rotation leads necessarily to the starting position, two rotations with different directions are required if one wants to obtain a different position, such as $1 \rightarrow 4$. These, however, cannot be anticipated and have to be determined by trial and error. This "required" necessity (the necessity of a new action, but whose procedure is still unknown) is well described by Iva, who begins by saying "I don't know (if I can get $1 \rightarrow 4$)," then tries $H \times R$ because *H* alone turns backward and two *H* lead "back to where it was." Similarly, And says that if one does not combine two rotations "at the same time, it stays in the same place." But even though this combination remains to be empirically discovered, the search is not determined by chance but is guided by a concern that is constantly present: that of coordinating the directions. Thus Jac spontaneously declares that to obtain $1 \rightarrow 4$ one has to do $1 \rightarrow 2$ and $3 \rightarrow 4$, even though the chip is invisible in position *2*, and only in position *4* has "it stayed [=come back] on the same side [visible]". Ste formulates more clearly this dual requirement: One has to "first lower the square and then turn." This shows the relationship existing between this type of necessity, which requires the composition of directions to be empirically discovered, and the other type described above of the chip's circular paths (without linear translation), which are linked to the rotations of the square to which it is attached. This relationship can explain the problem encountered by the 7-year-olds, in the beginning of level IIA, of knowing whether the directions are in part determined by the order and the direction of the rotations, as Nat assumes ("I am thinking about the direction"), whereas Dan recognizes the equivalences, as becomes general after 8 years of age.

Levels IIB and III

If Level IIA is characterized by the empirical search for combinations that are postulated as being necessary, but that subjects still need to explore in the directional transformations that they cannot yet derive by deduction, then one might expect that such anticipations should become systematic at level IIB. But, in accordance with what we have frequently observed, we are faced in subjects 9 to 10 years of age with apparent regressions, which are often surprising but which are of psychological rather than epistemological interest with respect to the problem of necessity. Therefore, we shall be brief in describing this phenomenon. In general, these apparent regressions are related to the fact that subjects discover new problems that they cannot immediately find solutions for. In the present case of composing rotations, there is a simple explanation: having understood the necessity of compositions, subjects no longer work at empirical explorations but try to anticipate everything by proposing all kinds of hypotheses. However, because they are not yet capable of understanding hypothetico-deductive necessity, their predictions follow the intuitions of the moment instead of being subjected to tests of internal consistency or any form of necessary control:

Aur (9;4) understands perfectly that one can *turn* R, H, *and also* R, but to return to the initial position she thinks immediately of the combinations $V \times H$, $R \times H$, $R \times V$. Since this leads to different results, she adds a rotation of the entire object, which is obviously equivalent to R: "Is it not the same if you turn it like R?" *Yes. I think so.* "You're not sure?" *Not really.* Having done $1 \rightarrow 4$, she believes that $1 \rightarrow 2$ is possible: *Since one can make it go there* [4], *it should be able to go there* [2]. She tries all possible ways, using again the rotation of the entire object. In spite of her failure, she maintains, for two chips in positions *1* and *2*, that the chip in *1* will certainly go to *4* but that the one in *2* will take its place $(2 \rightarrow 1)$. As for a third chip placed in the middle, *It will stay there, but I'm not really sure.* She keeps using this cautious formulation, following her initial failures.

Dil (10;5), at the first question about returning the chip, says *Sure, for example*, $V \times V$, *it comes back to the same place.* But that is not the only way: two R, two H one way or *the other way*, and, finally, *one can make everything turn*—meaning the rotation of the entire device, which is different from R because it includes the base: this leads to at least 10 different systems. As he does not manage to get $1 \rightarrow 3$, because that way the chip *is not in front*, he resorts to rotating again the entire device, placing it in a diagonal orientation. His failures do not prevent him from predicting, for two chips (in positions *1* and *2*), aside from the correct $1 \rightarrow 4$ and $2 \rightarrow 3$, the paths $1 \rightarrow 3$ and $2 \rightarrow 4$, with returns along the same parallel translatory paths, nor from believing that the center chip can change places.

It is not worth describing further the reactions of subjects who, having reached the stage of deductive thinking, consider all hypotheses possible. But because they are still completely insensitive to the need for controls, they fail to perceive their own contradictions—failing to generalize, particularly when going from one to two chips.

At level III, however, we find the regular continuation of the progress achieved at level IIA. Some of the 10-year-olds (and even an advanced 9-year-old) and all subjects between 11 and 13 solve the problems by simple deduction, since, exploiting the fact (discovered at level IA) that all paths described by the chip are rotations and that translatory paths are impossible, their representations of the chip's displacements allot the same importance to the invisible as to the visible side of the square:

Tho (9;3), after explaining the path $1 \rightarrow 4$ by referring to 2 on the other side, affirms the impossibility of the path $1 \rightarrow 2$ or the visible side: *It cannot get here* [2], *because it is on the same side. It turns like this* [V], *and when it has turned once it is on the other side.* "What about [$1 \rightarrow 3$]?" *No, because they are just on the side* [the same side]. He then shows the two visible positions, *1* and *4* and *in back, that one and that one* [2 and 3]. Therefore, he solves correctly for two chips also.

Tin (10;7), after $1 \rightarrow 4$ by $H \times R$, going through *3* (but on the back side), states for $1 \rightarrow 2$: *One can't, because if one turns* V, *that goes on the other side.* With three chips (*A, B, C*) placed in three corners (*1, 2,* and *4*), we ask where *C* would go. *There* [to *1*]. "Could it go [to *2*]?" *No, because one cannot turn the square like that.*

Car (11;0), concerning $1 \rightarrow 2$: *That doesn't work, because one cannot make a direct path* [translation]. "And that [$1 \rightarrow 3$]?" *Not either: if the other one didn't work, it follows that that one doesn't work either.* "Why?" *Those two* [$1 \rightarrow 4$ and $2 \rightarrow 3$] *go together; and those two* [$1 \rightarrow 2$ and $1 \rightarrow 3$] [drawn as rotations of positions 2 and 3 in back], *they also go together.*

Mac (11;11), after having demonstrated that $V \times H$ or $H \times R$, etc., *is always diagonal*, declares that $1 \rightarrow 2$ is impossible because *that* [the chip] *doesn't change place, it is only that* [the square] *that turns.*

Fra (12;0): Concerning $1 \rightarrow 4$: *I turn this* [V] *and I turn that the other way* [H]. "Is that funny?" *No, because we've changed that* [the direction]. But $1 \rightarrow 2$ is excluded: *One would have to go to the other side* [to see]: As for $1 \rightarrow 3$: *If one can't do that* [$1 \rightarrow 2$], *one can't do that either. I don't need to try.*

Every one of these subjects anticipates and readily carries out the compositions $V \times H$, etc., leading from *1* to *4* or from *2* to *3*. This needs no further illustration. The new phenomenon we observe is that the same operations (rotations) that render necessary the paths $1 \rightarrow 4$ or $2 \rightarrow 3$ also render impossible the translations $1 \rightarrow 2$ and $1 \rightarrow 3$. The progress from level IIA to level III consists, thus, in replacing the necessity of requiring an empirical exploration of the proper combinations with a deductive, operational necessity, predicting these combinations and excluding the impossible ones. The fundamental fact here is that the subject's geometry makes it possible to infer the different transformations in objective space. This gives them their logical necessity, which encompasses that of preceding levels, extending it and providing it with a better base by uncovering the reasons for each of these compositions or impossible combinations.

Conclusions

At this point we shall return to our initial question: In what way does space represent a particularly useful indicator of the isomorphic relationship between the necessities inherent in subjects' actions (from sensorimotor behaviors to the infralogical, spatial operations), and what can be postulated as being necessary about the spatial transformations in objects? In other words, what are the relations between the geometries of the subject and of the object?

We saw in the preceding sections that there is an interactive relationship that can lead to mutual disturbances if the relationship is insufficiently established but that can be mutually facilitating once this relation is well established. These interactions between subjective and objective space are apparently of a particular kind. They are much tighter than those between any kind of physical phenomenon and its causal model. The modest example of the data presented here, for levels IA to III, is only one particular case of a very general process linking the necessity inherent in subjective geometry to that postulated to exist in objective space.

Let us first recall that the subject is subject, at least from the moment she is born, in virtue of her intentionality and her awareness of her own actions, but that she is also object inasmuch as she is an organism performing material actions. These actions being spatial and directed at objects as well as at the subject's own body entails two fundamental consequences. The first is that the geometries of the subjective and of the objective world are basically of the same kind, no matter how diversified objective space may be in configurations and transformations and how simple the space of the subject with its primitive actions may be in the beginning. The second is that, as the subject's actions become internalized as representations and operations, the situation gradually reverses itself: because of the dual process of the formation of new possibilities and of necessities, the operational geometry of the subject becomes infinitely extended until it encompasses (sometimes even anticipates) everything science discovers about objective space, not to speak of those regions where it transcends scientific explanations.

It is self-evident that objective space has a role to play in this unlimited progress made by subjective geometry. Otherwise, one could not speak of interactions. In the facts just presented, it is the subjects' spatial experience that leads them, at levels IB and IIA, to discover what subjects are able to infer only at level III. In the development of scientific thought, there are many instances where problems of physics (the spin, Dirac's delta, etc.) have led to new discoveries in mathematics. But compared with the causal models of physical phenomena, the subject's assimilation of the forms and transforms of objective space represents a specificity not found in physics. Our research has shown for some time that, to perceive and to represent an order in a series of objects, it is necessary to use behaviors that are themselves ordered (a *counter*, as Berlyne said): look, touch, imagine, and so forth, in a definite order. In contrast, explaining the way a thermometer works or the effects of sugar in a glass of water does not require representations that are more or less warm or sweet. *Geometric intuitions* determine the type of demonstration to be given of a spatial characteristic; they take the forms and mimic their variations in an entirely isomorphic fashion with what can be read from the objects. In short, a configuration C or a transformation T of objects in space can be read only by means of forms C' or operations T' of a subject's geometry, such that $C' = C$ and $T' = T$. On the other hand, in any causal, not exclusively spatial model, the correspondence between the subject's operations and the object's actual behavior is always only approximate. Thus, space has indeed a particular role as mediator between the necessities characteristic of the subjects' deduced compositions and those that are to be attributed to the objects themselves, even more so and in a more general way than is the case with the principles of conservation, etc., that are common to physical and mental objects (see chapter 1).

Now this mediation is so remarkable that we have to ask ourselves whether it is not in contradiction with our general thesis, according to which necessity is a property of subjective composition whereas reality—and, therefore, among other things, objective space—can always only be assumed to be necessary. The facts described in this chapter show already at level IA a first kind of necessity (that of the return to the initial position by a semirotation in the opposite direction), followed at level IB by a second kind (return by a complete rotation), and at level IIA by a third kind (rotation of the chip itself, with exclusion of translatory motion). All three kinds finally come to be integrated at level III in the necessity of cyclical composition (which is no longer only postulated, as at level IIA, but anticipated by a deductive process), supported by explanations including that of such impossibilities as linear translations. Clearly, all this pertains to the subject's geometry; but why is it that we attribute only "necessariness" to the material apparatus and objective space? It would be too easy to say that the latter is a product of a subject's making, since the movements of stars and their compositions are analogous in nature and there is no reason to attribute them to Plato's deity, who "geometrizes" in all eternity (ὁ Θεὸσ ἀεὶ γεμετετ).

In actual fact, the laws of nature (including those pertaining to space) are only what they are, even though they are general and may be eternal. If one wished to find some form of necessity in them, one would have to try to reconstitute their history – that is, the processes of integration and progressive necessitation, assimilating the universe to an immense animal in the process of evolution; however, the universe is already completely integrated and ready to be necessitated (=interpreted as necessary). Possibility and necessity are, effectively, instruments of cognitive organization. They are operative in elementary behaviors of living organisms up to the most evolved forms of thought. They are not properties of what is only datum, however general it may be. Necessity cannot be found in nature and in space because there is no integration of preceding levels within later ones. This, however, is the main characteristic of necessitation in the realm of knowledge. In the physical world (as opposed to the biological), there is no analog to the developmental progression (at least not any more) if its laws are immutable.* In addition, reality is lacking in simultaneous co-possibilities of the kind the mind can encompass in their totality, whereas in reality, only one at a time gets actualized. Finally, the mind can look for and understand explanations by constructing models, whereas reality has only learned to know itself by giving birth (but only once and for all, so it seems, at least on this planet) to living beings and, through them, to the epistemic subject, to which we have to return in an inescapable circle (or spiral).

---

*In contrast, in biology one can speak of progression in the sense of an evolution of laws. For example, the laws of blood coagulation are not the same before and after hormonal regulations intervene, nor after regulation by the nervous system.

3

The Construction of a Slope

with C. Monnier and A. Boder

The problem posed to subjects in this task is to build three pillars, *A*, *B*, and *C*, out of equal-sized blocks in such a way that a wooden rail placed to run from *A* to *B* and another to run from *B* to *C* will make a single, long slope. A marble is then made to roll down from point *A* (but without giving it a push).* Thus, the problem is once again one of physical necessity, since the necessary and sufficient condition for the descent is that the pillars *A*, *B*, and *C* be constructed in decreasing order of height. But since the pillars must be assembled by the children rather than being selected from an already existing array, this apparently simple construction task requires the setting up of relationships. One point we wish to consider is whether one has to distinguish a procedural necessity based only on the sufficient conditions of success in this problem, or whether the necessitations to be observed are (as with the *explanations* analyzed in chapter 1) relative to the comprehension of the *reasons* for this success, and thus once again subordinated to models and their deductive compositions.

The method used induces from the start an attitude of comprehension; even though subjects are free to construct pathways as they wish, provided they get the marble to roll down from *A* to *C*, we start out by suggesting various constructions and asking for predictions and their justifications. For example, *A*=3 blocks, *B*=2, and *C*=1; or 3,3,1, 1,1,1, or 2,2,1, etc. In each case, we let the subjects test their predictions. When the marble does not reach *C*, we ask what could be done to correct that. Thus, we do not have a situation simply of free constructions, but rather an initial question period where subjects have to anticipate results, followed by the principal phase in which subjects have to correct constructions that include nonslanted pathways. This phase is of particular in-

---

*Both rails are 60 cm long (from *A* to *B* and from *B* to *C*), and the blocks are 4 cm high. The material is such that there is friction preventing the marble from rolling down when *B* and *C* have the same height, even after a fairly fast descent from *A* to *B*.

terest for the process of necessity formation (necessitation). In the last phase, which turned out to be rich in unexpected reactions, we ask for constructions or corrections when the height of one of the pillars is left constant and thus only two are subject to modification.

The problem to be treated in this chapter is, thus, one concerning physical necessity as related not to principles, such as that of conservation in additivity, but to simple integrative models of the relationships involved in cases like the construction of a slope by the seriation of heights in descending order of magnitude. The question of the relationship between necessity and integration is complex, and we shall frequently return to it. Necessity is to integration what possibility is to differentiation, which indicates the generality of the problem and its relation to the problem of equilibration. But, more specifically, we can ask whether necessity is the source of integration, by virtue of its organizing capacity, or whether it is the other way around—that is, necessity is the result of a synthesis of compositions. Or, alternatively, whether these two are inseparable aspects of a dialectical process of construction and necessitation. Let us approach the data without specific hypothesis, since the unforeseen diversity of incoherent reactions in a simple problem like that of constructing a slope with three pillars $A > B > C$ will show that the elementary integration of such simple relations as $<$ and $>$ already poses unexpected problems; this is what makes the following observations instructive.

Level IA

At around 2½ to 3 years of age, we observe a level where the slope has no necessary relation to the downward motion of the marble from A to C. The problem of integration is, at this level, simply one of learning, of coordinating the observed results. Here are three different examples of this:

Pau (2;5) tries 3,2,1 without a prediction, says *Ah!* [all surprised], and proceeds similarly for 3,3,1; he does 2,1, then 1,1 and 2,1; with the latter, he finally makes a prediction: *It's going to work.* "And 1,1?" *No.* "What can be done?" He does 2,2 and tries it out: *That doesn't work.* "What to do?" *Two, one.* He thus seems to understand, but still believes later on that 1,1 will also work and even goes back to 2,2. We return to three elements by proposing 3,2,1, where he sees the positive result after trying. He even corrects 2,2,1 to 3,2,1, of which he just saw the effect. But to see the failure of 3,3,1 he still needs to try, then "corrects" it to 2,3,1. Thus, there really is no learning evident until the end.

Bar (3;6) shows considerable progress in the course of the interview, but still without integration until the end. First she predicts of 3,2,1 that *that will work*, but the same for 2,2,1, which she "corrects" to 2,2,2, after having said, *No, it does not roll.* Since 2,2,2 does not work any better, she proposes 2,2,4: *I think that may work* She tries it. *No, it takes 2,3,4.* "That will work?" *Yes, because the marble is a bit big* [strong]. She then begins to understand by experience that *it can descend but not climb*. However, this does not prevent her from proposing 3,4,4 and 4,4,4: *I think that will work* [tries]. "What to do?" She tries 5,4,4. *That works a bit.* "So?" She tries 5,5,4. *That doesn't work.* We then again show her 3,2,1: *That will work: it descends all the way* [indicates this with her finger], but since 3,2,2 *doesn't work*, she "corrects" it to 4,4,2, then 4,4,4, as well as other combinations without a slope.

Yve (3;10): Toward the end, one observes some learning. We first propose 3,2,1: "Will that work?" *I don't know* [tries]. *It descended* [note the wording]. "And 2,2,1?" *Yes, it will go down* [tries]. *We have to put one here* [A]. "Or else?" *One here* [C]: Thus, 3,2,2. "That will work?" *Yes.* "And that: 1,1,1?" *No.* He does 2,2,2, then 3,2,2, then 4,2,2. "You can add or take some away?" *Yes, 2,2,2,* then 3,2,3, *because there* [3,2] *it goes down, and there also* [CB]. Noticing the mistake, he corrects to 4,2,2, then 4,2,3 and 5,2,3: *There* [5,2] *it goes down very fast* [wrong]. *Ah! we have to take the third away*; this gives 5,2,2, then 6,2,2, and he stops there.

These three cases illustrate a progression within what we might call integrative assimilation. Neither necessity nor even integration in the sense of a coordination of schemata or interdependent subsystems is present. At this level, we only find more or less adequate interpretations of observable facts and a form of integrative assimilation attempting to relate these facts to one another. Pau makes no reference to slope or descending motion, simply noting successes and failures, which he does not try to interrelate except from one trial to the next; neither is there any improvement in his predictions, nor any learning at any time of the interview. Bar predicts motion on a plane without a slope and even expects the marble to roll upward (2,2,4). She shows progress when she discovers that the marble "can descend but not climb"; however, she does not use this discovery and, in spite of the earlier failures with 2,2,2, still continues to construct level paths such as 4,4,4. Her learning thus does not include that of the opposition of descent versus horizontal path. Yve, on the other hand, shows a slight progress: even though not anticipating the necessity of the descent, he uses that term to describe the initial situation: "It descended." However, this still does not rule out level constructions like 3,2,2 or even 2,2,2. But in the end he demonstrates a clear, if imperfect acquisition: to enhance the slope 3,2,2, he raises A to 4; then he builds 4,2,3, which he corrects to 4,2,2; after some further errors with C, he comes up with 5,2,2 and finally 6,2,2!

Level IB

From 4 years on, subjects tend to predict or discover spontaneously that a slope is necessary to make the marble roll. Yet this schema does not suffice to ensure the integration of the constituent relations:

San (4;6): We set up 1,1,1. "Do you think that the marble will roll?" *No, it is too flat*. She constructs 3,1,1, and when she sees that this does not work, she does 3,1,3. "It will go?" *Yes*. "Where should it go?" *There* [C]. *No, it should go down all the way* [into the box]. *It cannot get to there because it goes uphill*. "So?" *I have to take one* C *away: 3,1,2*. "What does that do?" *I have to take away another* C. "And what if you do?" *I also have to take away a* B: *3,0,1*. "It works?" *I have to put two on* B: *3,2,1* [tries]. *It works: it goes downhill*. "And if you put one more on *B*, will it work?" *Yes, it would be downhill* [tries 3,3,1]. *No, it isn't*. "And if I put 2,2,1?" *No! No downhill from* A, *but from* B, *yes*. "What to do, if you only want two on *A*?" *Put one* C: *2,2,2. No, there would be no downhill*. "But can one change another one aside from *A* so it would work?" *No, one cannot. It takes two slopes*. "But if I change *B*?" *It would be flat*. She tries various ways, but only by adding blocks: 2,3,1 then 2,3,2 and 2,3,3. Finally she finds that one can take away one or two *B*: thus, 2,1,3, 2,1,2, and even 2,1,4. "That makes two slopes?" *No, only one* [2,1], *but starting from* B *an uphill slope* [1,4]. We then go back to 3,2,1: "What if I add one *A*, one *B*, and one *C* [i.e., 4,3,2]?" *That wouldn't work, it would be too high*. "And if I take away one *A*, one *B*, and one *C* [i.e., 2,1,0]?" *That wouldn't go: there wouldn't be any downhill*.

Cri (4;6), having explained that 3,2,1 works *because there is a slope*, predicts failure for 3,2,2 because *there is no slope there* [2,2], *and there is one* [3,2]. "What to do?" *Take away one* C; but instead of doing that, he adds one *B*, hence 3,3,2. "That will work?" *No, there is no downhill there* [3,3] *and no downhill there either* [3,2!]. Then he corrects to 4,3,2, which works, unexpectedly: *I see a downhill there* [4,3] *but not there* [3,2!]. "Are you sure?" *Yes, there is one*. Later he agrees that since 3,2,1 is alright, one can add one block to each: *That will go* [hence again 4,3,2]. But when asked if that is better, the same, or worse, he answers: *Better, because there are two slopes*. "Make a path so it will go as fast as possible." He takes off one block on each pillar, not seeing how he contradicts himself. "That goes faster?" *Yes*. "And can you make it roll very slowly?" *No* [but he builds 2,1,0: a new contradiction]. "And to prevent it from getting to *C*?" *You have to put three there* [2,1,3, without hesitating] *because there is an uphill slope*. "And if I want to leave three on *C*, can one change something so it will work?" *No*. "Try": he builds 4,1,3 and then 5,1,3, 6,1,3, and finally 7,1,3. "Would it be good to put some there [*B*]?" *Not at all!*

Fra (4;11) immediately demonstrates the descent for 3,2,1 and says that to correct 3,3,1, *One can take some away or add some more*, which does not prevent him from ending up with 2,3,1 and 3,3,3. "Will that work?" *No, it's very big, it has to be all low, quite tiny*: hence 2,2,2, 2,3,2, and 3,2,3. He indicates with his hands that the two slopes ↙ ↘ and ↘ ↗ go in the same direction; only later does he notice his mistake. Toward the end he improves his corrections:

thus, 5,3,3 to 5,3,2. But it will not work to add a block to each pillar, whereas taking one away would *because it will fall* [cf. *all low*].

Veg (5;1) for 1,1,1 begins by adding a block before *A*, then she does 2,1,1 and 3,1,1, up to 4,1,1. She rejects 3,2,1, which she changes to 3,3,1. Having tried that, she says, *There* [3,3] *it's straight* [=flat], *and there* [3,1] *it's like that* [indicating a descent with gestures]; this she corrects to 4,3,1, indicating the slope. This does not prevent her from trying to correct 3,3,1 (a configuration proposed) to 3,4,1 and, after that, 3,2,2 to 3,2,3, confusing the two directionalities. Toward the end, her corrections are appropriate.

Mat (5;6) corrects the proposed structure 0,2,0 into 2,2,0: *Otherwise, it will fall down* [from *B* to *A*]; then, *Look, I'll make it a bit taller and it will go all by itself* [3,2,0]. For 3,2,1, he says: *I believe that will roll quite fast because it's quite tight* [=steep]. In spite of these promising beginnings, he then accepts 3,2,2 *because here* [*A*] *it is high and there* [*B*] *and there* [*C*] *it is low.* He notes the error, and subsequently rejects even 3,2,1 *because before* [3,2,2] *it stopped.* When he tries he cannot explain the success, but then he accepts 3,3,1, which he then "corrects" to 2,3,1.

Dia (5;3) displays a similar odd mixture of momentary comprehension and lack of integration: 3,1,1 won't go *because there* [*BC*] *it's flat.* "So?" *It stays where it is.* "What is to be done?" *Make B higher*, hence 3,2,1. "And 3,3,1, that would work?" *Yes.* "Even if I put up three *B*?" *You have to put one more on* A. "And on *C*?" *Leave it as it is*: hence, 4,3,1. "If one adds one block to each pillar on 3,2,1?" *That would go better, because that* [4,3,2] *slides a lot.* "Why?" *Because it's higher.* But it would work also with 4,2,2 and 2,1,1, which she corrects to 2,2,1, and so on.

Mar (6;2) still corrects 3,3,1 to 3,3,4 and 1,1,1 to 1,2,1 then 2,2,1, etc. If one adds a block to each pillar on 3,2,1, *it wouldn't work, because it's too high.*

Isa (6;5) also considers the synonymy: *When it's low, it descends.*

Ser (6;5), while specifying that 3,2,1 works because it takes two slopes *AB* and *BC* and that *A* has to be *high, higher than* B, B *medium, smaller than* A, *and* C *all tiny*, still corrects 2,2,1 to 1,2,1, then 2,1,1, but is *not very sure.* He agrees that when adding one *A*, one *B*, and one *C* to 3,2,1 *it works*, but *faster*, whereas taking away one *A*, one *B*, and one *C it doesn't work anymore, it will be all straight* [=flat]. We demonstrate it at 2,1,0. *Oh, yes, it is about the same, but slower because there aren't three* A.

Cor (7;2) correctly changes 3,2,2 to 3,2,1 but does not believe that it can be done another way. "What if I give you more blocks?" *That wouldn't do any good: it would only make it taller so the marble cannot roll anymore.* Accordingly, she corrects 3,2,2 to 2,2,2 rather than to 3,2,1. *Oh no! It's all flat!* So she returns to 3,2,2, unable to suggest a solution, since *when it's high, the marble doesn't roll, and when it's all flat, it doesn't work either.*

We have given many examples because they are extremely instructive as to the conditions for integrating the system and thus for the appearance of necessities. An integrated system is characterized by two conditions, that of constituting a whole with stable properties (here $A > B > C$) and that of including compositions between its elements, which guarantee and conserve the properties of the total system. What characterizes level IB is that subjects are conscious of these properties but experience enormous difficulties in coordinating the relationships involved so as to create the compositions. In other words, they set a goal for themselves: "It takes two slopes," says San, who is only 4;6 years old; even "A must be higher than B, B medium, . . . and C all tiny," as Ser explains. The others only speak of "slopes" or simply indicate this with gestures, but all of them know what the general program is that has to be integrated. But as soon as they have to begin to carry out the compositions necessary for successful realization, the most surprising obstacles arise to interfere with and slow down this integrative process. Certainly, the seriation of three rods $A > B > C$ would pose no problem for these subjects. But in this case, they have to construct pillars out of blocks and even correct seriations that are proposed—that is, carry out transformations that are interdependent. Still, the small number (three) pillars and the simplicity of the goal, that of having a marble roll down from A to C, would seem to justify the assumption that subjects should not have any particular difficulties with this task. Yet, in fact, we do find considerable difficulties, and so we have to find out why these compositions are so difficult to realize.

The first explanation is naturally the fact that subjects do not anticipate, to a sufficient degree, the consequences of a substitution. This problem sometimes manifests itself only with respect to a single pair: Cor, even at 7;2, still corrects 3,2,2 to 2,2,2 (instead of 3,2,1), not anticipating what she notices only after the fact: "Oh, no! It's [AB] all flat!" Most often, this failure to anticipate consists in not foreseeing the consequences of one adjustment for the second pair of elements: San agrees that one can modify 3,2,1 to 3,3,1 because these would be "downhill [BC]," and concludes only after the fact: "No, it isn't [AB]." The lack of anticipation across pairs of pillars is almost systematic in the beginning of the interview and can lead to a false reading of the facts in the case of a fortuitous success. Cri corrects 3,3,2 to 4,3,2 to ensure the descent AB and does not immediately see that $BC = 3,2$ constitutes an analogous descent.

A second factor, less readily observed but more important than it appears, is that of false generalizations or analogies: San, having removed a block at C (3,1,2), concludes from this that "I also have to take away a B." Mat, having seen that 3,2,2 does not work, then rejects 3,2,1 "because before it stopped": that is, the first two pillars (3,2) remain identical in both situations.

On the other hand, the opposite can be observed with regard to both successive and distant items. In fact, it is rather surprising how little subjects make use of previous experience to solve new problems. Thus, Mat and Dia initially perform surprisingly well for their level, but then regress to the usual kinds of errors. Cri thinks that the marble will roll faster where the stacks are very high, but then he produces very low stacks to make it go "very slow." He is not aware of his own contradictions. In short, it is a fundamental fact that solutions found previously (let us call them as a whole the *no longer problematic*) determine, to an incomplete degree only, the solutions to follow (=the ones that are *still problematic*). In contrast, the origin of necessary deductions is the complete integration of prior acquisitions within new problem situations.

A fourth factor is involved in subjects' failures: the lack of coherence between what precedes and what follows frequently leads to subjects' forgetting (in the course of the action) the general orientation $A \rightarrow C$, in spite of the fact that they had identified this initially as the plan to follow. Thus, Fra, Veg, and some others offer solutions $A < B > C$ or $A > B < C$—that is, with two descending slopes but in opposite directions—while gesturally indicating a single direction. The reason for this is undoubtedly that children frequently attempt to verify a series *ABC* by visual scanning in both directions. This otherwise quite legitimate method of verification then leads to a result at variance with what it is meant to accomplish.

A fifth negative factor is the difficulty (which is quite general in all domains of preoperational thought) of conceiving of a set of transformations as co-possibilities. Subjects act as if they consider a solution (correct or incorrect), once it is identified as correct, as the only one possible. This lack of mobility is, of course, related to the insufficiency of anticipations (factor one), but has to be distinguished because it has to do with the dynamics of possibility. The most striking example of this is Cor's behavior, who even at 7 years of age discards both a series she considers too high and a horizontal one (rightly so), and then fails to see the possibility of correcting 3,2,2 by taking away one *C* (=3,2,1).

Related to this lack of co-possibilities is a sixth factor—that of false absolutes, or a failure to use relational concepts. Thus, these subjects never speak of "higher" or "lower," but only of "low" (Fra's "all low") or "high" (Cor: "When it's high, the marble doesn't roll"). Particularly, when reading and causally interpreting the facts, not one of the level IB subjects understands that if one adds to or subtracts from each stack one block, the slope does not change and the relative differences between the stacks remain the same. Therefore, they expect different and often contradictory effects from one case to the next: if one makes them higher "that won't work, because it's too high" (San, Mar, and Cor); or, on the contrary, it would roll better and "faster" (Ser and Cri, before contradicting himself). Taking away one block from each stack would make it go better (Fra and Isa) or worse to the point that there would be no slope at all (San with 2,1,0) or more slowly (Ser with 2,1,0 also). Recall also the absolute value attributed to *A* by Cri (near the end) and by Veg, as they let $B < C$ or $B = C$ (Cri allows $B=1$, even with the series 7,1,3, believing that it would be useless to make B higher).

This lack of relativization leads to a seventh and last factor of great importance, which we call *pseudonecessity*. In fact, there is a difference between not understanding that the slope remains the same when the same number of elements are added to or removed from each stack (A, B, C) because of the absence of relational concepts and believing that the best slope is necessarily the highest or the lowest one with respect to the ground level, since this limits the co-possibilities and orients the corrections in a specific direction (adding rather than subtracting or the other way around). But mainly this reveals the incomplete and erroneous nature of the necessity attributed to the movement of the marble. All subjects at level IB understand that this movement is determined by the slope produced by the difference in height between the pillars A and C—in other words, $A > C$ (this is progress compared with level IA). But the reason perceived for this law is only that it is easier for the marble to "slide" down a slope than to climb up or stay in place, as expressed by Dia. However, what these subjects are prevented from seeing by the existence of such pseudonecessities is that the speed of the marble depends on the amount of difference between A and C and not on their absolute height. This explains the systematic error of the type: it "slides a lot . . . because it's higher," as Dia remarks.

Before proceeding to level IIA and the main problem raised by it, let us note that although the subjects of this next level often succeed in freeing themselves of these pseudonecessities, there are many examples of residual functioning of this kind in 7- to 8-year-old subjects:

Sab (8;2), with 2,1,0: "If one adds a block each to A, B, and C, would that work?" *I don't know* [in the following, only finds 3,2,1]. "And if one subtracts a block from each?" *That would work.* "How?" *Not as well, because it is a bit lower.* "And if one adds a block to each [i.e., 3,2,1]?" *That would work just as well.*

Nia (8;6) immediately corrects 4,4,4 to 4,3,2 as at level IIA. "And if I add one block to each?" *That would go better, because it's higher.* "And if one takes one off each pile?" *That would work*, but again *better*, before concluding: *It would be the same.*

Ria (8;5), for 3,2,1: "If one takes one off each, would it work?" *Yes* [confidently, because of 2,1,0]. "Same speed?" *Slower, because here* [$A=2$] *it's lower.*

Dra (8;6), for 3,2,1: "If one adds a block to each pile?" *That wouldn't work. . . . Yes, it would,* "How?" *Better, because it's higher.* "What about adding five to each?" *That would work.* "How?" . . . "And if I take one off each?" *That would still work because B is lower than A.*

These intermediate cases show progress in relational concepts, but also the resistance of the initial pseudonecessities.

Level IIA

The sublevel characteristic of 7- to 9-year-olds raises a new, interesting problem with respect to the mechansims involved in integration—that is, in the process of necessity formation. Subjects at this level succeed more or less rapidly in correcting the series to the form $A > B > C$, as long as the three pillars can be modified at will. However, they still encounter considerable difficulties when one of the three is proposed as invariant and the two remaining ones need to be adjusted to the fixed pillar:

Dom (7;2), for 3,2,2, begins by adding one block to A and notes that with 4,2,2: *It doesn't roll like a marble*, which should keep the momentum gained from $A=4$ on 2,2. He concludes immediately: *It takes another one on* A *and* [hesitating] *one here* [on B, confidently]. "Why?" *Because with four* A, *three* B, *and two* C, *I'll always have a grade*. We present 3,2,2, and this time he proceeds by subtraction (note the co-possibilities): *I have to take one off there* [$C=1$] — *No, because there are three* A *and three* B. *That's flat*. "So?" *Take one off here* [B] — *No, I have to take one off there and there* [B and C, that is, 3,2,1]. For 4,2,2, *I have to take one here* [C] *and leave the other two; so there* [AB], *there is a steep descent* [four A and two B] *and there* [two B and one C], *there is a smooth one*. For 3,3,3, he proposes 3,3,2 and immediately corrects it: *Remove one there* [B] *and one there* [C]. "That will work?" *Yes* [3,2,2]. *No, I have to take two off here* [C] *and one there: there will be two descents* [3,2,1]. But in spite of the rapidity with which he responds, he is lost when asked to leave C unchanged for 3,3,3: He only finds 4,3,3, then 5,3,3. "And if I don't want more than five in A?" *You have to take one off here* [C, thus 5,3,2]. "But if we don't want to touch C?" *Then, it isn't possible*. We have to make the following suggestion: "And if I put one there [B]?" *Oh, yes, that makes 5,4,3*. "The number of blocks is important?" *Yes, the number*. "What is more important, the number of blocks [i.e., the absolute height] or the path?" *It's enough if it slopes down*. Thus Dom attains relativity, freeing himself of pseudonecessity.

Alb (7;6) corrects 3,3,2 to 3,2,2 and then immediately to 3,2,1. With 3,2,2, he says immediately: *We have to take one off at* C. "Could one do something else?" *One can try different ways*. He builds 3,1,2, but says immediately: *Ah, no*, and corrects to 5,2,2 and then immediately to 5,4,2. "And with less?" He builds 4,3,2. "What if one takes one off each?" *Always the same, because all are lower*. But when we set $A=2$, unchangeable (2,3,2), he removes one C and puts it on B, producing 2,4,1, then removes three B, obtaining 2,1,1. He needs to try it before finding the solution 2,1,0.

Nad (7;4) corrects 3,2,2 to 3,3,2 and 3,2,1. With 3,3,1 and B fixed, *I have to take one* A *off* [$=2,3,1$] *because I'm not allowed to take one off* B.

Ben (7;11) easily corrects 2,2,1 to 3,2,1. "And if we don't touch A?" *It doesn't work, because if you have one more here* [C], *it would be flat*. "And there [B]?"

No, because here it's flat [AB] and there it's sloped [BC]. "And if one doesn't add to *A?*" *That will never work.* "Would it be good to take one block away?" *That doesn't do anything!* Still, Ben attains relativity with small differences. For 3,2,1, "If you put one more block on each?" *That would work as before* [immediately], *that would be the same thing: 4,3,2.* "What if you put one less block on each?" *Yes, like now.* But with 10 more on each pile, he regresses: *That would work, but slower, because it is higher.*

Bel (8;0) immediately corrects 3,3,1 to 3,2,1. She agrees that adding one block to each of 4,3,1 would work, that it would make 5,4,2. "And if I take one away from each?" *Yes* [confidently]. But to correct 3,3,1 by leaving *B* unchanged: *That isn't possible.* "Why?" *Because if one takes off at A, then it will roll down the wrong side. Here [B], it's not allowed, and here [C],* removing one] *does not change anything.* We then suggest that she add something, and she answers: *Add one there* [to *A*]. "Sure?" *Not quite.* "One can do something else [with 3,3,1]?" *Take one there* [from *C*], *that would be the same as putting one there [A]. Ah, no! there [AB], it's straight* [=horizontal, and judged as such, as if 3,3 could not change if *B* is left invariant]. "What is to be done?" *There is no other way.* For 2,3,1, she responds immediately: *Add one* [to *A*] *– no, two, otherwise it is all straight* [=flat]. "And if we don't change anything here [*A*]?" *Yes, take away two there [B], that would work* [=2,1,1]. "One or two?" *One, ah, no, otherwise there will be two left like there [A, and it wouldn't roll. We can't add anything here [B] or else the marble will turn around.* "So?" *It's impossible.* "Why?" *If I take two off B, it would be low and all straight* [flat between *B* and *C*]. *Perhaps one could take one off* [2,2,1] *or perhaps two* [2,1,1]. "One cannot touch *C?* *If one takes one off here [C], it would always be from the highest to the lowest [BC];* so that would not change anything!

These observations are rather surprising. As long as they can modify all three pillars, the subjects, even though not succeeding right from the first trial by using purely deductive thinking, still find correct answers rather rapidly. Compared with level IB, there is definite progress: more anticipations, fewer false generalizations and contradictions, more consistency between solutions already found and future responses. Principally, the new acquisitions are of two kinds. They affect the fifth and seventh factors described above: the appearance of co-possibilities (see Dom, as well as the "different ways" foreseen by Alb for the same series to be corrected) and, in certain cases, the relativization of the slope with respect to absolute height ("It's enough if it slopes down," says Dom; similarly Alb and Bel). This eliminates the pseudonecessities of the kind "lower" (or "higher")=better descent (Always the same, because all are lower," as Alb says). This being so, what remains problematical is that, as soon as one pillar has to be kept constant, everything goes wrong and the same subjects regress to level IB: Dom does not think it possible to correct 5,3,3 if one leaves *C* unchanged and if one does not go beyond $A=5$, as if $B=4$ were not entirely obvious. Alb, with 2,3,2 and A constant, takes off one C and puts it on B, since he cannot put it on A. Nad, similarly, with 3,3,1 and B fixed, only succeeds in taking off one A "because I'm not allowed to take one off B," neglecting or forgetting the necessity $A > B$. Bel, with the same series 3,3,1 and B invariant, can only think of removing blocks without adding any and finds the solution impossible, as if blocking B would simultaneously block the equality three A = three B and a reduction in C would have no effect with respect to the coordination AB with BC. Another subject, Ben, only thinks of adding, never of removing blocks.

Our problem is thus to explain these erroneous reactions, which are characterized by the idea that the fixed element is no longer part of the game and that only the two remaining elements and their interrelations are taken into consideration; these reactions are illustrated by those of Alb, Nad, and Ben when they carry out, on the adjacent elements, the changes that would have to be done on the fixed element. On the other hand, we find the opposite idea, as when Bel believes the relations between the mobile and the fixed element to be blocked, since the fixed element has to remain as it is. The reason for these difficulties seems to be a lack of reciprocity in the transformations establishing the appropriate relations between the fixed and one of the other elements. When all three elements are variable, a desired relation such as $A > B$ can be obtained either by making A larger or B smaller, according to the converse $B < A$. This makes six possible transformations, $<$, $>$, or $=$ in either direction (AB or BA), only two of which are correct and four to be eliminated. It is important to consider both these directions, since subjects can anticipate or check the series by scanning it either as $C < B < A$ or $A > B > C$. When A is fixed, however, only three transformations remain open, since only B can be changed to obtain $A > B$, only one of which is correct. The new problem is thus to reconcile a more restricted number of possible transformations with the necessity of referring to the fixed element. It is undoubtedly this absence of mobility and reciprocity that constitutes the main difficulty of these questions: to be able to change only B to obtain $A > B$ is obviously less convenient than to be able to carry out two possible transformations, $+n$ on A or $-n$ on B (or both). In general, if all three pillars can be modified, a total of 18 transformations are possible, of which 12 must be eliminated (only 6 are correct: $A > B$ or $B < A$, $B > C$ or $C < B$, and $A > C$ or $C < A$); this caused a difficulty at level IB that was overcome at level IIA. But if one element is constant, only 12 transformations remain, of which 8 must be eliminated; and of the 4 that are correct, 2 are inconvenient because of lack of reciprocity.

Level IIB and Conclusions: Integrations and Necessities

As early as 9 to 10 years of age, subjects solve the problems with three variables by purely deductive anticipation and no longer by a mixture of inferences and empiricism, as at level IIA. Similarly, the situations with fixed elements are mastered:

Lau (9;4), with 2,2,1, removes one *B* then *C*, thus: 2,1,0. "Is it the same speed as 3,2,1 [presented on trial 1]?" *That amounts to the same, because there was only one less to take away.* For 3,3,1: *We have to either add one there [A] or take one off* B. For 4,3,3: *We have to add one there [A] and one there* [on the second]. "And if you want to make only one change?" *Take off there* [the second pillar: *3*].

Oli (9;5), 2,2,0 with *B* fixed: *We have to add one* A *and one* C. "You have to?" *No, one on* A *but not on* C. "And if you leave three *B* on 2,3,0?" *You have to add two* A. *If you add only one it would be flat.* "If you put up 10 *A*, what can you do to make the marble run down as before, with 3,2,1?" *Put up nine* B *and eight* C. "Is that the same?" *Yes, also 2,1,0.* "And if you let *A*=1, with 1,3,2?" *That wouldn't work, because then we would need zero* B *and then it isn't possible with* C. "What is the minimum for *A*?" *It's two.* "And if I add a rail?" *Then you would need at least three* A.

It is surprising that such responses appear as late as this. Yet, this fact is interesting with respect to the relation between necessity and integration. There are two kinds of necessity implicated in this research. The first, which we have not tried to analyze further here, is physical: it is the necessity of having a slope in order for the marble to descend. At level IA, this condition is not yet necessary: the marble is "big" enough (=strong), as Bar says, to climb from 3 to 4; only experience teaches her that the marble can only descend. But from level IB on, the subjects, like San, declare that the marble will not roll on the "flat" and that with the material used "it takes two slopes" (A→B and B→C); Ser puts it more precisely by saying that *A* must be "high," *B* "medium," and *C* "all tiny." Even though this comprehension adds a certain kind of necessity to the simple generality arising from the reading of facts beginning at level IA, the resulting model only amounts to relating the movement of the marble to its spatial context and no longer simply to an inner driving force: on the flat nothing can move it ahead, but on a slope an upgrade constitutes an obstacle, whereas a downgrade makes it "slide a lot" (Dia). Later, subjects invoke weight, and so forth, but this is not relevant here.

The second form of necessity, the only one studied here, consists of discovering and satisfying the necessary and sufficient conditions of descents and correcting the arrangements proposed when these do not correspond to the system, which is accepted at level IB − in other words, $A > B > C$. These corrections, which are constantly required, derive directly from the process of necessitation, since the necessity of p can, in general, be recognized from the fact that non-p would be contradictory; in this particular case, the relations to be corrected are contradictory with the law $A > B > C$. Levels IB and IIA teach us that it is one thing for a subject to understand the holistic nature of a system (e.g.,

$A > B > C$) but quite another to master the compositions that bring about or respect these holistic properties. We are thus in a position to identify the relations between the progressive integration of a system, the process of necessitation, and necessities as compositions, the inverse of which would be in contradiction with the law.

A system is, as was specified above, a set of interdependent relationships constituting an entity with stable properties, independently of the possible variations of its elements. A system can thus function via actions or operations, which temporally and successively modify its elements. It further incorporates a *structure* — a nontemporal set of possible transformations — that preserve the holistic characteristics of the system. We shall designate the construction process as *integration* and its final stage as *integrated*. *Necessitation* consists of those successive compositions that render necessary certain relations generated by the integrative process (for example, the composition of descents $A \rightarrow B$ and $B \rightarrow C$, which were first established separately). The term *necessity* describes the atemporal status of the result of these compositions, where their negation (or absence) would be contradictory with the laws of the system.

But to understand the relations between necessity and integration, let us distinguish three possible dimensions that the facts observed have established. The first is that of *determination*, a search for the necessary and sufficient conditions for obtaining a given result: for instance, that A must be higher than B to assure a descent from A to B. The second is *analysis*, which consists in giving the reason for a transformation to be performed: for instance, with 1,3,2, A has to be made higher or, to produce a slope, one has to set $B=0$ (Oli). Finding the reason amounts to motivating and justifying the determinations. Its importance within the process of necessitation also derives from the fact that the reason invoked then generates a second reason, a reason for the reason: thus, Oli further argues that if B is reduced to 0, then there cannot be a descent between B and C. More analysis then leads him to the conclusion that A cannot be less than 2. The third dimension involved in necessity is a kind of *amplification* in the form of implications: if A, B, or C is constant, then . . . (see the preceding section); or, in Oli's case, if with two rails A cannot be less than 2, then with three rails it must be at least 3.

Given these statements, it is obvious that necessities are required in the process of integration, if only to ensure that the transformations involved conserve the characteristics of the total system. But a system may also contain nonnecessary compositions: to conserve the descent $A > B > C$, the differences between A, B, and C need not be equal: integrations are thus more inclusive than the necessities they imply. Necessitation, on the other hand, always leads to integrations, since it is the result of compositions that cannot remain isolated. But since each necessity generates new possibilities and since its analytic and amplifying characteristics constitute in and by themselves a source of new developments, it follows that necessitation with its consequent integration (i.e., the construction of a system) tends to enlarge the old system by creating a new one, which includes the preceding one. In this respect, each necessitation is richer in the possibilities that it implies than the system within which it is integrated at any particular moment. It follows that there cannot be any interaction between the process of integration within a system S and one or the other necessitation N, where SN represents the part common to both, S non-N the nonnecessary transformations of the system, and N non-S the possibilities going beyond S and constituting an opening toward a new system S'. Thus, since S cannot become integrated within S' and since SN becomes extended to $S'N$, one can say that it is the integration of the old within the new that essentially constitutes the foundation of necessity; without such a process, it may happen that the systems S, S', etc., could become contradictory or incoherent.

These considerations seem to be borne out by the facts presented. They show, first of all, that the three distinct forms of necessity—determination, analysis, and amplification—constitute three stages in the process of necessitation. At level IA (where subjects do not postulate a slope), we observe the beginning of determination (necessary conditions) deriving from both empirical statements of fact (Bar's "it can descend but not climb," after having predicted the opposite) and semi-inferential processes derived from the subject's action: a purely spatial reading of a slope would require complex referencing procedures, whereas assimilation to one's own actions (it is easier to run downhill than uphill or on the flat)* is probably involved in the interpretation of observables and in the early predictions of level IB (prediction preceding the actual construction of a descent). At level IB, thus, we find determination as to the general form the system has to take but incomprehension of the component operations because of a deficiency on the analytic dimension—that is, an incapacity to understand why some solutions work and others do not. Level IIA, in contrast, constitutes a nice illustration of analysis (reasons for the compositions), yet with no amplification in the case of fixed elements. Finally, we have amplifications at level IIB, when subjects solve this problem and various others (that of equivalence classes like 2,1,0 and 10,9,8 in Oli) and even that of going from the system S, with two rails, to another, S', with n rails.

We thus observe a close relationship between these particular stages in the form necessity takes and those we described as compositions that are both integrative and necessitating. The aspects that are proper to the process of integration can be found in the continuous transitions from external variations to those intrinsic to the system. At level IA, the empirical, external aspects are largely

---

*Very young children believe that an identical distance is shorter when downhill than uphill (see J. Piaget, *Les notions de mouvement et de vitesse chez l'enfant* [Paris: Presses Universitaires de France, 1946], chap. 4).

dominating and the beginning of integration amounts to little more than relating observables (registering results); there is as yet no system. A first system emerges at level IB with the formulation of the law of the total set (descent from A to C). But there is still no composition other than by trial and error, no adequate anticipation: external aspects still predominate. Only at level IIA do transformations become oriented toward internal aspects; they are derived, in part, by deduction, by subordinating the particular relations to the law of the whole. Finally, at level IIB the internal aspects predominate, which indicates that the system is integrated — that is, the entire structure is reconstituted as a result of compositions, just as the latter can be inferred from the structure. In a word, integration, as an organizing process, is the source of necessitation, which, in turn, acts as a stabilizing force ensuring that integration is balanced and simultaneously acting as amplification, thus making augmentative changes possible.

4

Necessities Involved in Length Measures

with E. Ackermann-Valladao and K. Noschis

Chapters 1 and 2 dealt with factors relating the necessities resulting from the compositions carried out by the subject to the "necessary" properties inherent in objects, and chapter 3 has focused on the relations between necessity and integration. We shall now combine these two aspects by examining measurement and formulating two new questions. One is of the conservation kind, more precisely additive conservation as necessitated by measuring lengths; this is no longer simple commutability as discussed in chapter 1. Rather it has to do with *connectability*, or automorphous correspondence between the parts *a, b, c* . . . of some measurement scale—length in this case—and the same parts after a transformation in shape or orientation that conserves their connections in terms of adjacencies. The other question is whether there exists a kind of necessity that is specifically procedural or whether what appears to be such can be reduced to structural necessity, since procedures can be successful even if they are limited to the "sufficient" without requiring the necessary. The latter may thus be implicated only in the comprehension of the "reasons" for successful or unsuccessful outcomes. This would bring us back to the structural aspects.

The problems revised here with respect to necessitation are rather different from those that guided our earlier researches on the problem of measurement, as carried out by one of us with the collaboration of B. Inhelder and A. Szeminska,* where some of the behaviors to be described below have already been presented.

The length comparison is to be made between line segments placed on a sheet of paper in different positions. The segments, which are presented in pairs, can be straight lines or in zigzag formation. After an initial perceptual estimate, subjects are asked to measure the segments, using as a standard pieces of flat

---

*See J. Piaget, B. Inhelder, and A. Szeminska, *The Child's Conception of Geometry* (New York: Basic Books, 1960).

spaghetti that subjects can cut as they please. The eight configurations used are shown in the accompanying drawings. The task is formulated as follows: "There

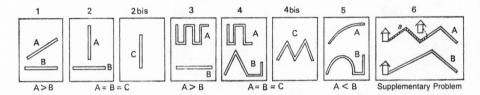

are two roads [the experimenter points out the two segments to be compared]. Can you tell us if one is longer, where is it farther to walk [etc.]? How do you know? Can one be sure? What can one do to be really sure?"

In each case, the experimenter asks for a judgment, a justification, and a verification; then, if the subject does not resort to measuring spontaneously, the experimenter suggests using the standard, noting all the procedures used by the subjects on each trial, their gestures and so forth.

In situations 2 and 4, a third segment is introduced to question the child about transitivity in the case of simple figures and with complex figures. We also ask children to construct paths of equal length to be evaluated on the two paths of situation 5.

Level IA

As we know, these initial preoperational reactions include neither conservation of length nor transitivity. Consequently, there is no spontaneous or even solicited use of measuring tools. But what interests us here, as regards necessity, is not so much the deficiencies as such but the criteria subjects use to evaluate and characterize length and particularly to what extent these criteria are related to each other in terms of composability. Since compositions include necessity as an inherent property, the first stage in the process of necessitation or integration (which determines it) in any domain would be to make the initially heterogeneous criteria comparable and composable. In the case of length, level IA shows us that this goal is not at all achieved: the criteria used have very little coherence indicating just how much remains to be acquired before the necessities inherent in measurement are finally developed.

Dim (5;0), in situation 1, judges the oblique line *A* to be the longer one, and in situation 2 it is the horizontal one that wins (the only reason given: *I thought it out in my head*). The experimenter measures them by fitting the spaghetti to *A* and aligning it with *B*: *They're both the same length*. But this comprehension is not accompanied by transitivity or conservation. To test for the former, we add a vertical segment *C*, and Dim judges *C*=*A* as *A*=*B*, but *C*>*B* (after the display is hidden) *because I just saw it*. To test for the latter, we line two spaghetti pieces *a* and *b* against each other and then push *a* forward; Dim judges *a* to be longer because it goes farther than *b* on the right. We place *a* in zigzag formation and *b* becomes *longer, because it's straight*. In situation 3, *B* is judged *longer because it goes there and there* [stands out at either end]. We suggest that he measure the segments to see how much he understands: he makes *B* twice as long by joining a spaghetti, then breaks one up to cover parts of *A* and, while doing this and again at the end, declares: B *is longer*, without any comparison between the measuring tools. In situation 6 he pays no attention to the zigzag formation and puts a house on *B* directly underneath the one near *A*.

Lou (5;5), in situation 1, says that B *is longer*. "Sure?" *I don't know*. "One could use the spaghetti?" *Yes*. He takes a long one and puts it between *A* and *B. Those two are small*. In situation 2, *B>A*. "Sure?" *Yes*. "I would say *A>B*." *You're right. No, I am: it's easy to see*. The experimenter demonstrates measurement. *The two are the same because the spaghetti did not stick out*. But in situation 3 he simply puts a spaghetti over *B* without shifting it to *A*, and he concludes: B *is longer*. When we add *C* to situation 2, Lou fails to show transitivity: *One can't tell*.

Nad (6;11) shows no understanding of conservation (the extending segment=the longer one, the zigzag one=shorter). In situation 2, the horizontal line is longer *because there is farther to walk*. When asked to take a measurement, she sticks the spaghetti close to each of the two segments without comparing them. In situation 3, *B* is longer *because A goes like that* ↓, *like that* →, *and like that* ↑. Length is thus seen as depending on position.

Pat (6;4), in contrast, sees the vertical segment in situation 2 as *longer, because it goes from the bottom to the top*; but after the experimenter's demonstration, she agrees that they are *the same length*. However, in situation 1 (presented here after situation 2), the horizontal segment *B* is *longer*. "Why?" *You can see it*. To prove it, she places two spaghetti pieces on the segments: when she finds that the spaghetti on *A* is too long, she concludes from this that the oblique segment *A* is *longer*. "Why?" *Because the spaghetti goes farther* [!], which shows the sense she makes of the adult notion of measurement.

Xav (7;4) does not conserve when two elements, *A* and *B*, are changed from congruence to a staggered configuration. In the first case, *You can see they're the same length*; but after staggering, *B is bigger, because you've moved it ahead*. "But what would it be like for an ant that crawls?" *A is longer, it's farther in back*. We leave *A* horizontal and set *B* at an angle of 60 degrees to *A*: *A is longer: it's straight;* B *is more tiring, because it's a triangle, a hill*. In situation 2, *There isn't one that is longer: the two are the same length because they're both straight*. In situation 1, A [oblique] *is longer, because it's a bigger road*, also, *it goes uphill*. In situation 3, A *is longer because it's completely straight*. Xav does not use the measuring tools.

Ean (7;11), in situation 2, measures by hand but does not conserve distances in transposition well: hence, $B > A$. In situation 3, B is *longer, but if you make* A *longer* [linearly], *then they would have the same distance to walk*. In situation 4, B *is longer because there are more zigzags*. Then he counts: four segments in B against six in A, *but* A *is still longer, even if it has fewer zigzags*. In situation 5, B *has less far to walk because he makes zigzags*. But when situation 4 is presented again, he symbolically sweeps one spaghetti piece alongside A, then puts it aside and does the same for B: he compares them and notes that the spaghetti pieces are the same length (obviously, since he did not cut them); hence he concludes that $A = B$, even though to the eye A remains longer.

These facts inform us about one aspect of necessity, that of *determination* — the necessary and sufficient conditions for the use of a concept. In length estimation and comparison, determination consists essentially in quantitative composability in the sense of additivity, either numerical or geometric. Such compositions determine the sense of the notion of measurement. Even in the case of nonnumerical measures (those that are devoid of proper units of measurement) of the kind that we ask subjects to carry out with the spaghetti, the comparison between A and B becomes quantitative in this additive sense as soon as the subject understands that the length A includes length B plus a part that is added, which implies that length B is a part of length A. Therefore, there has to be homogeneity between the lengths to be compared and, in general, between the different comparisons to be made; otherwise the *more* and *less* would only refer to quantitative variations that cannot be composed in additive fashion.

Precisely such heterogeneity characterizes level IA, where length is evaluated only as a function of shape or orientation without any notion of a partitive, additive hierarchy. Thus, Pat estimates the vertical segment to be longer (situation 2) "because it goes from the bottom to the top," which reminds one of a well-known optical illusion. But most of the subjects (Dim, Nad, Lou, and Xav in the beginning consider the horizontal in situation 2 as longer because it is "straight" (Dim), flat and "farther to walk" (Nad). In situation 1, the oblique segment (which is, in fact, shorter) is at times judged shorter because of the privileged status of horizontal lines, but at other times longer (Dim, etc.) "because it goes uphill," hence "a bigger road" (Xav). The same subject, Xav, even arrives at certain contradictory conclusions for identical configurations, depending on whether he thinks of how "far it is to walk" (i.e., how "tiring" it is) or of what it looks like (perceptual judgment): using the former criterion, the angular path, the "hill," and the oblique line are longer; with the latter, the horizontal is nevertheless the longer one because it is straight. Similarly, in the frequently used criterion of which line extends farther (which may suggest the notion of parts and additivity), most subjects consider only the point of arrival and pay no attention to the point of departure. They thus confuse a quantitative notion of length with a perceptual one. Xav even goes so far as to say that when the segments are staggered, *B* is longer "because you've moved it ahead" (=extension); but to an ant that walks on it (which focuses attention on the point of departure), *A* is longer "because it's farther in back." Zigzags are generally judged as shorter than the horizontal to which they are compared, but still they may be considered longer because of the greater number of segments involved.

This lack of additive composition of length can thus explain in a natural way the absence of any sense of measurement as well as of conservation and transitivity – of any necessitating composition. When the children are given the pieces of spaghetti, they never use them as middle terms; rather, they place them over each line to be compared as if doubling the lines would make them easier to evaluate. But this is not at all true. In fact, subjects often neglect to break the spaghetti pieces to adjust them. They then compare, as does Pat in situation 2, the line *B* with the spaghetti on *A*, which is too long; so, *A* becomes "longer" "because the spaghetti goes farther." It is true that when the experimenter does the measuring in situation 2, the subjects conclude that there is equality. They do not apply this to other situations, however – they do not transfer their measuring stick from one segment to the other – and since in situation 2 measurement reveals only equalities and subjects do not yet understand transitivity, their conclusion that *A*=*B*, may be caused by perseveration rather than by deduction and understanding of necessities.

Level IB

The following subjects show various kinds of progress in quantifying length. We shall try to find out what all these reactions have in common.

Nic (6;0) says in situation 1 that *B* is *longer because the bar is more flat.* In situation 2, he traces the lines with his finger and concludes that *A*=*B*. "Sure?" *I think so.* "Can you use the spaghetti to be more sure?" *Yes.* He breaks up a spaghetti to place it over line *A* and then line *B*. *A is longer.* "Sure?" *Yes.* "Did you need the spaghetti?" *No. You can also do it with your fingers.* We demonstrate the transfer of the measuring device: *But the two are the same length!* "How do you know?" *You put the same piece of spaghetti on* A *and on* B. We introduce *C* (=*B*=*A*), and Nic applies the spaghetti, cut to fit, to lines *A* and *B*. When asked whether *A*=*B*, *B*=*C*, and *A*=*C*, the answer is: *It's the same. I remember.* In situation 3, he lays one spaghetti over *B* and cuts pieces for the segments of *A*, but he stops in the middle: *In any case, I know it already;* B *is longer because it's straight and it goes farther.* In a situation similar to 4, but where *B*>*A*, he traces *B* with his finger and then begins doing that with *A*, but then says: *I already know,* B *is longer than* A. "How do you know?" A *is more folded, so it's smaller.* We present a *C* (>*B*): *It's bigger: I saw it with my finger.* We ask him to recall *B*>*A* and *C*>*B*, asking if *C* is longer than *A*. He responds in the affirmative and justifies his answer. Still, one may hesitate about attributing true transitivity. It may be simple repetition of the term *bigger* of the kind he used for equalities (*I remember*). In fact, Nic does not conserve at all. When a line is bent to /\ , he declares that it is longer *because it's straight and because it goes farther*. When the original shape is restored, he finds that *they're both the same*.

Mag (6;8) similarly fails the conservation questions. In situation 2, she turns the paper by 90 degrees as if trying to judge independently of position. She considers *B*, which is vertical in this position, to be longer. Then she puts the paper in the original position. This time she considers the vertical line *A* to be longer: *You can see it's bigger, and it is bigger*. We suggest using the spaghetti, and she places one on *A*, another one on *B*, and compares them. As soon as we take them away, she falls back in her contradiction: once *A*, then *B* is longer: A *is the biggest, I can see it, but normally* [simulates measuring] *I know it's* B [the spaghetti extended a bit] *and when I turn it's the same*. In situation 3, B *is longer*. "Sure?" *Yes, I can see it*. "And with the spaghetti?" She covers *B* with a whole stick of spaghetti and *A* with pieces that fit more or less, which she then applies to *A*. *That's funny. This time it's that one* [A] *that is longer. I said it is* B, *but that isn't true. It's* A. *I know it*. We take the spaghetti off: *It's* B *that's longer*[!].

Syl (6;5), in situation 1: *They're both the same*. "How do you know?" *You have to look at the length* [and not at the direction!]. But in situation 2, *It's* B *that is longer* [*B* is horizontal]. "Could one use the spaghetti?" She aligns them with *A* and *B* without transfer. *Of course,* B *is longer*. The experimenter aligns the spaghetti on *B* with *A*: *Oh, it's the same thing!* "So?" *By looking one can see that* B *is longer, but in length it's the same*. We add *C* to test for transitivity, and she concludes that *B*=*C* from *A*=*B* and *A*=*C*: *They're the same length*. "And comparing *A* with *B*?" *It's* A *that's longer*. Situation 3: B *is longer because* A *is all broken up into little sticks, and that one is big*. She places one piece of spaghetti over *B* and fits pieces for *A*, but makes no transfer. "Is that good for something?" *Yes, that is good for seeing the length*. Situation 4: *They're the same length. It looks like* B *is longer, but they're both the same length*. "What makes you say that?" *Nothing*. "And with the spaghetti?" She covers the two lines, but without transfer. A *is longer. We've seen it with the spaghetti*. "How can you prove it?" *With my fingers* [repeating her previous tactics without transfer or additivity]. We add *C*, which is equal to *B*. She concludes from *B*>*A* and *C*=*B* that *C*>*A*, which is authentic transitivity, accompanied by conservation: *They are the same because just now it was the same* [congruence]. However, in situation 6, she reports the distance *a* from *A* to the path *B* (i.e., equality), but concludes that *the same path is a lot longer* [in *B*]. Thus she does not conserve what she measured!

These intermediate reactions attest simultaneously to an adherence to a length concept understood as a qualitative form (level IA) and attempts at integration in the direction of a concept of homogeneous quantity (level IIA) that is susceptible of additive quantification. Many residues of qualitative form evaluation are still evident: segments are considered longer when they are "straight" or "flat" (Nic) or, just the opposite, vertical (Mag); if they are made of little sticks instead of being "big" (made of a single piece) (Syl) or not "folded" (Nic); and particularly if they extend beyond the other segment at the point of arrival (this occurs generally in situation 6 or on missed conservation questions).

In other cases, we observe certain efforts to get away from form to homogeneous quantification. Among these the most noteworthy is the spontaneous use of one's fingers as a measuring device, which tends to homogenize one situation with respect to another. It also amounts to a consideration (at least in action) of the interval between endpoints rather than merely the extension at the point of arrival. A second noteworthy element can be seen in Syl's remark in situation 1: "You have to look at the length" and thus disregard the direction of the segments to be compared (which, however, is not generalized to situation 2). Still another indication is Mag's behavior, when she rotates the second paper by 90 degrees to compare horizontal and vertical positions; this does not prevent her, however, from believing that the same object can have two different lengths (a frequent reaction at the intermediate level): A in vertical position being longer, whereas in horizontal position it is shorter. As for additivity, it begins when Mag transfers to B the small pieces of spaghetti (situation 3) placed over the segments of A (as opposed to Syl, who fails to transfer the pieces).

This leads us to consider the reactions to measurement as proposed by the experimenter, which are very instructive in their complexity. One extreme reaction consists in simply placing the spaghetti over the segments to be measured, as Nic did at first without any transfer from one to the other or any comparison of the measuring standards to each other, their being detached from the lines to be measured. But subjects recognize readily that this procedure is not at all necessary and that one can do it just as well by using one's fingers. The second extreme reaction consists at this level, not yet in resorting to a spontaneous use of measurement, but in comprehending it when it is observed and in subsequently adapting it at least partially. Nic, as he watches the transfer of the measuring standard from A to B (in situation 2), understands immediately but with surprise that $A=B$, whereas he had previously judged $A>B$. Then he uses the same method to compare C and B. But later on, in situation 3, when it would be really helpful, he gives it up again. Between these two extremes – from total incomprehension to at least local comprehension – we observe behaviors of great interest for their partially integrative character: the result of measurement is accepted, but this acceptance does not exclude direct evaluation that is contradictory with it. Thus, Mag applies measurement herself by transfer in situation 3 and concludes: "That's funny. This time it's [A] that is longer. I said it is B, but that isn't true. It's A. I know it." Then, once the spaghetti pieces are removed, it is B again that is longer. Syl, whose remarkable distinction between quantitative length and qualitative forms and orientations providing different size criteria we described above, maintains and even accentuates later on this difference, which is essential for the integration of the various individual lengths within a homogeneous whole: after measurement in situation 2 (but with the transfer of the standard carried out by the adult), she concludes: "By looking one can see that B is longer, but in length it's the same." Then she specifies that measuring "is good for seeing the length." One might expect that she would give priority to the latter, but in fact this is not the case. Rather, two types of size concepts continue to coexist, both considered valid in spite of their contradiction. In situation 6, she measures correctly the distance a on A (relative to the position of the house) and also transfers it correctly to B; but then she infers from this, without any qualms or hesitation, that the second segment b (b on B, equal to a on A) makes a path "a lot longer" (because of B's longer extension, since B contains a single angle and A contains three). There is thus no conservation of the measured entity, even though she had given successful conservation and transitivity responses.

This intermediate level IB shows clearly how complex the relations are between necessity and integration (as discussed in chapter 3). Integration begins as soon as subjects search for a homogeneous criterion that is common to all the various qualitative forms of length (the only ones considered at level IA). Sometimes this development is induced by the measures proposed, at other times it comes about spontaneously. Still, these efforts at integration remain partial, leading in fact to two main subsystems: that of qualitative length of shapes and orientations and that of quantitative length susceptible of conserving additivity. The latter only begins to appear at level IB.

Level IIA

At about 7 to 8 years of age, at the beginning of concrete operations, a general integration of the sense of quantification begins to constitute itself, contrary to Hegel's law (true in other domains) of the shift from quantitative to qualitative change. These advances manifest themselves in the generalization of *transfers* to ensure proper measurement, in subjects' search for linearity (transforming zigzags into straight lines), and in certain cases in explicit additivity:

Nat (7;6) begins with level IB reactions. In a situation similar to 3, but with $A > B$, she first judges $B > A$ because it is straight; upon suggestion, she uses the spaghetti, placing a whole one over B and another one over the four segments of A but without marking them. Hence, she concludes that A is longer. How to be sure? She then cuts four segments corresponding to those of A and lays them over B, which is a definitely additive procedure. In situation 4, she superposes segments on both A and B, but it does not occur to her to arrange the two sets of spaghetti into two straight lines that can be compared. Still, she says: *I'm try-*

ing to imagine what they would be like if they were in a straight line. Before, it was easy because the lines were straight. This explains her judgment that $A > B$ because *A has more pieces.* The same argument is used in situation 5 ($B > A$), but following an overall measure with a thread.

Ste (7;9), in situation 1, measures first with his hand and concludes correctly that $B > A$. *You can also see it if you turn the paper: they start at the same place* [horizontal reference] *but B goes higher.* In situation 2, he does spontaneous measurement with transfer: *They're the same length. That surprises me: B seems longer* [the well-known optical illusion]. He measures the segments of *A* and aligns the measuring sticks parallel to *B*: *I put them down in a row, because I could not unfold* A[!] In 4, he measures the segments of both *A* and *B* and aligns the two sets of measuring sticks in two parallel straight lines. We present another configuration, with *A* as in situation 4 and *B* in a series of eight zigzag lines: *Well, A is bigger.* "How many pieces does it have?" *Four.* "And in *B*?" *Nine: You tried to get me. But the bits here* [B] *are tiny. Altogether they do not even make one piece of* A. Ste understands transitivity for equality, but he gets mixed up when presented with three unequal, irregular shapes.

Uro (8;4), in situation 2, measures spontaneously using spaghetti. In 3, he uses a single spaghetti, turning it at each angle and adding up without error the lengths of the segments one after the other. Then he compares it with another spaghetti piece placed over *B*. "What if you didn't have two spaghetti, but only one little piece?" *Yes, that helps* [too]. He correctly identifies the units and counts them. In 5, *I imagine it* [A] *straight, straighten it out. It would be about the length of this paper. With* B, *it would go up to there, then I add that and that* [straight segments]. We present two simple curves: he invents a flexible measure, using his index finger, which he bends over each curve to identify their lengths.

The notion of length as an additive quantity thus definitely wins out against the qualitative notion of shape and orientation. This brings about a certain number of necessitating compositions that, however, are still accompanied by uncertainties and gaps. We can note five kinds of advances at this level, as compared with level IB. The most important advance is the homogeneity of all comparisons based on a single notion of length in general. No longer do we observe the incoherent and contradictory statements that inevitably arise when the evaluations vary with observable perceptual judgments. Thus, Ste may find that in situation 2 "*B* looks longer," but he no longer distinguishes the two subsystems found at level IB—the subsystem of lengths that "one sees" and that of lengths verified by measuring. He only considers the latter as valid, the former as illusions: "It only looks it."

The second advance is in the use of a single, unitary criterion: the length of a path is defined as the interval between the endpoints of a segment measured by following its path irrespective of its shape or orientation. Thus Ste, in situation 1, turns the paper around to make one of the endpoints of *A* and *B* coincide and to find that *B* extends at the other end. In situation 6, the house in *B* is no longer seen as being underneath that of *A* but as being the same distance from the endpoint, as measured by taking into account the turns and by ignoring apparent overshoots.

Third, when the forms to be compared are heterogeneous, subjects make up for this by a reduction to linearity: "I'm trying to imagine what they would be like if they were in a straight line." (Nat) and "I imagine it straight" (Uro); even better, Ste carries out partial measurements of the segments in situations 3 and 4 and then "puts them down in a row" to compare their sums, since he cannot "unfold" *A* or *B*.

Hence, fourth, we have the fundamental property of length: its conservation of additivity, which means that the total length of a path is the sum of the partial lengths of its segments. All subjects reconize this. Better still, where the measuring device is a "tiny" bit of spaghetti that is used as a unit, length is seen as the sum of successive and counted applications of this unit of measurement on all contiguous parts of the path to be measured.

This leads to the fifth point, which may seem relatively unimportant but is essential from the point of view of necessitation and measurement. Since length becomes a common and homogeneous property, hence an abstraction, subjects can understand that if $A > B$, the length of *B* is part of that of *A*, which amounts to saying that $A = B + x$, where x is the added difference. Thus, for Ste, "the bits here [*B*] are tiny. Altogether [additivity in *B*] they do not even make one piece of *A*."

We shall come back to the necessitating reasons in these advances when discussing level IIB, which completes what is missing at level IIA. Even though all subjects of level IIA conserve length and understand the transitivity of simple equalities, they still fail to comprehend transitivity with three complex, unequal figures.

Level IIB and Conclusions:

From 9 to 10 years of age, transitivity appears to be understood as logically necessary in all situations studied (aside from one or two transitional errors).

Mic (9;9), in situation 1, begins by evaluating the unequal extensions at *both ends* and correctly presumes that $B > A$, but *one would have to check by measuring*. He does so, correctly transferring. In situation 2, he says: A *is longer than* B, *but since there is not much difference, one has to measure*, hence $A = B$. We add $C = B$. "And between *A* and *C*?" He laughs and immediately replies: A *equals* C. In situation 3, he measures the first segments of *A*, compares these with *B*, and concludes that $B > A$. In situation 4, with $B > A$, he pivots the standard about the angles, comparing from *A* to *B*. We propose a *C* of the form

⋀⋀, which he measures and concludes that $C > B$. We remind him that $B > A$ and $C > B$ and ask about the relation between C and A. He replies: *Obviously, C is longer than* A. *No need to measure that—it has to be* C *longer than* A.

Lil (9;6), in situation 3, cuts a spaghetti into lengths corresponding to segments of A and compares them with B, and in situation 4, reuses the same unit n times. Transitivity is obvious, as with Mic.

The acquisition of this form of transitivity between heterogeneous figures marks the final stage in the construction of length conservation, where length exists independently of any changes in form or orientation. Thus, this is the time to ask where this conservation comes from, which opposes additive, quantitative length to qualitative length and which is at the origin of the advances observed when subjects attain level IIA. The conservation of length quantities constitutes a prototypical example of a necessity n, since its negation non-n results in contradictions, as the reactions at levels IA and IB clearly show; it now remains to establish how the subjects of level II liberate themselves from these contradictions. In other words, we have to ask what the cognitive or compositional bases are that enable subjects to discover the necessities that were completely unknown before.

When the changes in the form of an object are caused by a displacement of parts of the object with respect to each other (as in the clay ball test, etc.), conservation is recognized when the subject understands that what is added at one point is equivalent to what is taken away at another point—when the problem of the invariance of the whole is replaced by that of the conservation of displaced parts. This problem is relatively easy to solve because it is based on the simple notion of compensation. In contrast, when the changes in the form of the whole do not concern separable parts and when neighborhoods are conserved (as with a line when its form is changed), conservation is said to be acquired when the subject recognizes that the segments are still the same, as well as their connections, but that they have only changed orientation with respect to one another. In this case, we shall speak of *connectability*.* In this case, also, the problem of conservation involves a transfer from the whole to the parts, and it is similarly simplified by the fact that their interconnections help to make them stable and that a change in the overall configuration can be reduced to local changes in the relative orientation of adjacent, connected segments with respect to each other. This is what is not comprehended at level IB, when Nic affirms that a straight line is longer than its corresponding angular shape but that they will be equal again if the latter is unfolded. The subject only considers the form as a whole without decomposing it into its interconnected parts. In contrast, all subjects at level IIA reason in terms of substitution of positions: Nat tries to imagine what

---

*See the beginning of the chapter for a definition of this term.

the angular paths in situation 4 would be like in a straight line; Ste aligns his standards in parallel, straight lines "because I could not unfold [the measured items]"; and Uro, in situation 5, straightens A by "imagining it straight." Each of these subjects conceives, thus, the differences in the shape of the whole in terms of substitutions of positions of segments relative to other segments. Therefore, conservation becomes necessary because of subjects' ability to perform compositions on the basis of parts that they have come to see as interconnected. These, like the commutable ones, integrate the parts within a total system of displacements. In this case, the substitution of positions (a kind of compensation in the large sense) plays the role of compensations between parts that are taken away at one point and added at another, characterizing the conservation by commutability. In addition, the connections between successive parts are the result of an automorphic correspondence that relates a whole or a sector to its adjacent parts, independently of its directions.

Measurement requires conservation of both the measuring tool and the objects measured (see Syl in situation 6 at level IB). As such, it is based entirely on connectability: whether it is a matter of reducing an irregular line to a linear segment or of using a series of connected units without gaps or partial overlaps, it amounts essentially to comparing two segments A and B of any form whatever by means of a middle term, M. This requires a transitivity that results from a double connectability between A and M and between M and B. This explains its generality (starting at level IIA) in the case of simple forms and its late appearance (level III) in the case of more complex forms, which make it more difficult to apply connectability.

This brings us to our last problem: does this structural aspect of measurement suggest that there is a procedural form of necessity distinct from the structural one, or rather, is the latter the only kind of necessity? In the first place, one may suppose that the qualitative length concept of level I will develop into a quantitative one only under the influence of a measuring procedure that is invented to make up for the perceptual inadequacies. But our conclusions from the foregoing analyses seem to go against this proposal by showing that measurement itself is possible only after the concept of length has undergone certain necessitating transformations, since measurement requires conservation and transitivity. In fact, this is only a special case of a situation of great generality: there is a distinction to be made between procedures as bringing about successful performance and the reasons accounting for performance (successful or unsuccessful), as understood by the subject. Performance requires only sufficient conditions, not obligatorily necessary ones, whereas the comprehension of reasons involves structural necessities that depend on progressive and finally permanent integrations of systems, especially the complete integration of what gets superseded within the new system. In the present case, we find that already at level IA, where length depends on forms and orientations, two segments may often be correctly evaluated as equal or unequal and, in every case, the whole is always judged longer than its parts. There is, thus, in spite of the very considerable differences between levels continuous development in the process of quantification. This development involves successive extensions of initially local necessities the result of *elaborations* (comprehension of reasons). The final product is connectability, which makes measurement possible. There is no doubt that procedures play a very important part in mental development.* But their specific contribution is that of generating new possibilities rather than of logical necessities, which only come about through structural comprehension of reasons.

---

*See the research currently carried out by B. Inhelder and her team on strategies in general. B. Inhelder, E. Ackermann-Valladao, A. Blanchet, A. Karmiloff, H. Kilcher, J. Montangero, and M. Robert, "Des structures cognitives aux procédures de découverte," *Archives de psychologie*, 1976, no. 171, pp. 57–72.

5

Associativity of Lengths

with C. Coll and E. Marti

In dealing with the question of the necessities proper to associative compositions, we raise two important new problems. Operational compositions, even in their concrete organizations, are necessary but in two different ways. The first has to do with their coordination as' structures, such as *grouping, groups, trellis*, and so forth. If we had proposed to study the necessities internal to each of these, we would only have repeated our previous structural analyses. Such redundancy was to be avoided by all means. However, other general forms of operational compositions exist, such as the associativity of additions or multiplications, and distributivity with or without commutativity. Their general property is to be common to several *structures*, which gives them the character of *constitutive coordinations* or, if you prefer, of *pro-structures*.* For example, associativity conditions numerical additions and multiplications: $(n_1+n_2)+n_3=n_1+(n_2+n_3)$, etc. It is also present in the case of substitution classes: $a+(b+g)=(a+b)+g$, or A^1 (a =the relevant class)$+A'_1$ (=the remaining subclasses a and b)$=A_2$ (=g)$+A'_2$ (=the others, 1 +b). Finally, it is necessary in the addition of length, which we shall study here. These pro-structures have their proper closures, or, with Bourbaki, their *stability of operation*: an associative series of three elements when composed with other terms gives another associative coordination. Thus, and for convenience, we shall use systems of four or six elementary lengths and also vary the forms to better attain those pro-structural necessities that are the objective of the first of our new problems.

This problem gives rise to a second one. If the associative composition of the various segments to be added leads to the conservation of closed systems, then we must ask whether it is the conservation of this system that necessitates that of the components or whether the process goes in the opposite direction. The preceding chapter has documented the heterogeneity of criteria used to

---

*The prefix *pro-* here denotes preparation.

define an elementary length concept. This justifies the formulation of the hypothesis according to which the conservation of an associative whole (which may therefore be divided into different subclasses, keeping their order and number constant) plays a dominant part in the conservation of its elements when these take on different orientations. More precisely, we shall call *elements* the invariant line segments of various lengths that compose our figures; we shall call *parts* the variable subassemblies of elements forming subsets within these figures; and we shall call *whole* the sum of all elements synonymous with the set of all subsets. Then we shall ask whether the conservation of the whole, when the parts are modified, derives from the invariance of its elements or the other way around; or, alternatively, whether the two go together—that is, the variability of the parts presents obstacles to both the conservation of elements and of the whole.

In addition to these general questions about associativity, we introduce a supplementary problem. This makes all the more interesting the fact that correct solutions appear quite early, coinciding with level IIA (7–8 years of age), as described in chapter 3: length being constructed as a homgeneous, additive quantity as opposed to a qualitative length evaluated according to shape and orientation. The novelty of our supplementary problem is the following: when we wish to distinguish parts within an identical whole—for example, $(A+B)+C=A+(B+C)$—we shall not simply use vertical bars symbolizing the separations (AB/C and A/BC), but we shall replace these bars with cuts (AB . . . C and A . . . BC). In this way, subjects have to carry out the addition of parts mentally—in a way, inferentially. They are thus deprived of the perceptual facilitation afforded by contiguity of the line segments A,B, and C. This additional difficulty increases when both the elements and the parts in our total figures change orientation.

Methodology

We have used two complementary methods. The first consists in presenting subjects with a certain number of line segments (strings held together by pins) of various fixed lengths. These we call *fences*. In the beginning, both the experimenter and the child receive such a fence, two identical open and continuous figures (no separations). The figures are exact replicas of each other in terms of positions, lengths, and so forth. Somewhat later, the experimenter cuts her figure in one or two places, creating different parts within her whole; then she does the same to the subject's figure but chooses different places for the cuts, resulting in different parts. The child is then asked whether the two paths, which were initially identical, continue to be of equal length, and if so, why.

Experimenter (A)   **Child (B)**

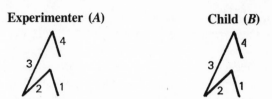

Each segment (*bit*) is of a different color. The two fences, *A* and *B*, are identical. They are constructed in front of the child, who is invited to compare each pair of segments. Then the following question is asked: "If I take a walk like this [describing the whole path *A* with one's finger] and you take a walk like that [tracing the whole path *B* with one's finger], would both of us have the same length to walk or does one of us have farther or less far to walk than the other?"*

Experimental variations (the same question is asked in the following situations):

A-1. Identical number of cuts in different places:

A-2. Variation in the spatial disposition of elements between figures:

B-1. Different number of cuts introduced in the two figures:

B-2. Different number of cuts and different spatial disposition of elements in each figure:

---

*If, with this demonstration, the child erroneously believes that the lengths to be added include the intervals between segments, we suggest imagining an insect walking on the fence that flies over the gaps from one segment to another. Only the latter are to be considered as being part of the walk.

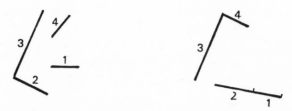

With some subjects, we followed a shorter procedure. First, the child notes the equality of two strings (the experimenter's and her own) arranged in identical zigzag patterns by means of a few pins:

Experimenter   **Child**

Throughout the experimental session, the task is always to judge whether the two fences have identical lengths in the different situations. A first modification is then introduced: each fence is cut once at different places (for example, see *A*-1). The modification is repeated, but one fence is cut in more places than the other (for example, see *B*-1).

The second method may appear rather different from the first because it uses *enclosures* (closed figures). The transformations consist of various kinds of openings or changes of form. The conservation of the total length of the perimeter is guaranteed by the fact that the same string undergoes all the transformations (as 7-year-old Cat remarks, "It's the same string, but not the same design: yes, the string cannot become smaller and smaller or longer and longer"). The following new question is added, more complex but interesting from the point of view of associative additivity: of three differently shaped enclosures, *A*, *B*, and *C*, two are merged into a new unit (with the perimeter $A+B$) of a new shape; the three components remain isolated from each other in the corresponding set. The problem thus presents itself as follows: $(A+B)+C=A+B+C$? But however different this task may be from that of the fences, both contain the necessary connections that characterize associativity: given two totals, *T* and *T'* formed from the same elements *E* and *E'* that can be distributed into different parts *P*, would $T=T'$ remain true since *E* is constant in spite of the variations of *P*? Both tasks incorporate not only dimensional variations but also directional ones (otherwise, with a single-directional straight line, the problems could be solved too easily by simple perception), as well as form variations in the case of the enclosures. But, in this case, the problem $T=T'$ remains the same and the correct solutions will be all the more valuable because they are made less obvious and all the more

interesting because they coincide with the level where the concept of length becomes free of qualitative criteria.

In situation 1, we begin with two identical, closed shapes formed by four
strings 10 cm long, each of a different color; then certain variations on openings
are introduced. For example:

$$\square = \square \ ? \quad (a) \ \square = \square\!\diagdown \ ? \quad (b) \ \square = \square\!\diagdown \ ?$$

$$(c) \ \square = \square^{+} \ ? \quad (d) \ \square = \square^{+} \ ? \quad (e) \ \square = \text{---+--+---} \ ?$$

In situation 2, variations are performed on closed figures. For example:

$$\square = \square \ ? \quad \square = \triangle \ ? \quad \square = \triangle \ ? \quad \square = \triangle \ ? \quad \square = \square \ ? \text{ etc.}$$

In situation 3, compositions of lengths, we begin with six figures that make
up three identical pairs (same color, same length, same form):

The following compositions are explored:

$$(A+B)+C=A'+B'+C'?$$

For example,

$+C=A'+B'+C'?$

$$(A+B+C)=A'+B'+C'?$$

For example,

$=A'+B'+C'?$

$$(A+B)+C=A'+(B'+C')?$$
For example,

$=C=A'+$ $?$

Constructing Fences

Level IA

The heterogeneous and contradictory comparisons of lengths characteristic of level IA (as reported in chapter 4) naturally recur with an additional difficulty – that of joining the separated pieces. Thus, level IA is characterized only by subjects' total insensibility to these contradictions and the absence of any quantitative length concept in the sense of additivity.

Jul (5;2) already at *A*-1 denies the equality of the figures that were identical at the start: *Mine is longer, because it is like that* [cut (1) + (2+3+4)] *and also mine is not cut there* [between 3 and 4]. "If you don't count the gates?" Jul traces with his finger the two total paths. *Yes, it's the same because you do like that and me too* [shows the total outline and the angles, then points to the two endpoints]: *Yours is almost there, and mine too.* We present the elements of the two fences as parts (1+2+3)+4 and (1)+(2+3+4), arranged in two parallel, straight lines but not exactly aligned: *Mine is longer* [extends farther]. We align them: *Now, they're the same.* We go on to *A*-2: *That one is bigger, because it has more gates.* We align the four elements of both the experimenter's and the subject's set as four horizontal lines, grouped as (1) + (2) and (3) + (4): *Yours is longer because you have many barriers, and I have only one.* He makes 3 out of it, but (3+4) is much longer than (1) and (2). Then the experimenter arranges her segments in one long, straight line and invites the subject to do the same with his: Jul uses the same starting point, but without any attempted measuring, and arranges (2+3+4) as a connected line that he manages to make extend beyond the extreme end of the other: *Yes, mine is bigger because I have that end here* [as it was decided by him in advance].

Pat (5;2), with a single figure of three elements (a Z with an extended baseline), declares, for a gap between 1 and 2 and between 2 and 3 in the respective figures, that *they have the same to walk.* When asked if she could make hers bigger, she closes the gap and arranges her elements in continuous fashion (⌐___), saying that in this way the walker *does not stop there.*

Cri (6;1) understands well that there is as far to walk on one and the other of the starting figures because one *walks on the same fences.* But as soon as the pieces are cut, he introduces the notion of speed, contradicting himself as follows: *If it's cut there, it goes faster* [jumps] *and that goes on*; or: *That isn't as fast, if it is not cut, one can keep on going* [does not have to stop]. Some other criteria: it is farther to walk *when it's all straight* or depending on how far the endpoints are *apart.*

Oli (6;2) thinks that it is farther to walk *if there are more holes*, but does not know why. Somewhat later, he affirms the opposite without giving any reason.

He thinks only of the cuts and not of the intervals between the ends (elements or parts).

Pra (6;2) similarly indicates equality of length in the initial figures, even specifies this segment by segment; but for *B*-1 (the only situation studied), he declares that *yours is longer because there are more holes*. Later on he says the opposite but does not justify it.

It would be useless to give more examples or details of the long interviews conducted, since chapter 4 has already documented the contradictory variety of forms of what we have called qualitative length. What is new here is that the comparisons require additions between discontinuous segments separated by cuts (parts) or between contiguous segments forming an angle between them (elements). What is noteworthy is that there is no additivity in the responses, either of equality (given at one time by all subjects and based on the analogy of the overall form) or of inequality (by far the most frequent response). The reason for this lack of additivity is that the cuts here do not serve to determine quantitative lengths or to mark border lines but only to interfere with the continuity of the path, eventually to affect the speed of the walk or simply to determine the number of components without distinction between elements and parts.

As for nonadditivity, Jul first agrees that there is equality between figures because of common actions ("you do like that and me too") and when the endpoints of the two figures converge ("almost there"). But then he definitely denies equality when we align the components, and additivity could be reduced to a simple, perceptual reading. As for the cuts, when subjects are asked to lengthen their paths, they constantly react by eliminating them because that way, as Pat says, the walker "does not stop" or, as Cri says, it "goes on": thus, continuity becomes an index of length, in particular "when it's all straight." The inverse also holds: the cuts may be considered as making the path longer, "more holes," which implicitly means more pieces. Many other criteria may be used, such as, for inequality, the degree of openness, the surface covered, the endpoints; or, for equality, the endpoint, the number of cuts or components. But there is consistent absence of additivity, which goes together with the lack of a quantitative length concept in the sense of chapter 4 and the incoherent diversity of criteria.

Level IB

The new reaction at Level IB is seeing the cuts not simply as modifying the relations of continuity but as delimiting length, which thereby becomes susceptible of addition. However, what is still missing for these additions to conserve the whole is the notion of compensation between the parts—in other words, comprehension of the fact that an increase in one is always accompanied by a decrease in others. Such comprehension would make the emerging additions conserving:

Ovi (5;3) first agrees that there is equality in *A*-1 *because it's cut here and there* [(1+2+3)+(4) vs. (1)+(2+3+4)]. But he changes his mind by judging his figure as *bigger*: *That is a big piece* [2+3+4]*and that* [1] *is small, and on yours, you have one bigger piece* [1+2+3] *and one small one* [4], which, of course, seems to be an instance of compensation. He appears to agree when asked if that makes the same whole: *Yes, I think so* [not very sure]. He regresses when asked whether one could make one of them longer: *Like that* [he joins his 4 with the set 1+2+3], *it's bigger now*. Similarly, in *A*-2, he denies equality because the figure on the left has more cuts. "What to do to make them the same length?" *You have to put them together* [not the additive expression] *here and there* [1+2 and 2+3] *and leave that* [3+4] *as before*.

Fra (6;3) denies equality in *A*-1 *because you take that* [2+3+4] *and I take that* [4] *and that* [1+2+3]. *And that* [1 on the left], *you leave it all by itself.* "But I take the whole thing." *That's not the same because you have cut there* [(1) (2+3+4)] *and that isn't very long, and here* [1+2+3] *that is long.* "But all that and all that together—it doesn't make the same?" *Yes, if you put back* [group] *that and that* [the separated components]. "And if one leaves the cuts?" *It's not the same because* [on one side] *you take that piece there* [2+3+4], *and on mine it's only that* [4]. This goes on for a while until the question is asked: "And what if I take that and also that [i.e., the whole]?" *That makes the same*, Fra finally concedes. But soon he contradicts himself again by saying that, if one puts in another cut, *that makes less, that does not make the same fence* [total length]. In *B*-2 he seems to have regained his comprehension when he says that in this case there is equality and if the two cuts are *not in the same place that doesn't change anything*. But with one cut more on one side, the result is that *mine is longer*. When the experimenter aligns her elements [1+2+3+4] and asks Fra to do the same with his, he traces a long line [1+2+3] by making a rough estimate and adds 4. The whole comes out considerably too long (as for Jul at level IA).

Xan (6;8) agrees that there is equality in *A*-1 and makes a comment concerning this equivalence that is worth quoting: *You can't have one that's the same* [as the other] *and not the other: they both have to be the same, else you can't do it*. With the six-element figures, we insert a cut at [(1)+(2+ . . . +6)] in one figure and at [(1+ . . . +4)+(5+6)] in the other: he classifies these parts into *small here* [1], *big* [(1+ . . . +4)] *and there the biggest* [(2+ . . . +6)], specifying that a cut that makes smaller [(1)+(2+ . . . +6)] [in one part] *and bigger* [in the other]. Nevertheless, the figure [(1)+(2+ . . . +6)] *has more string than that* [(1+2)+(3+ . . . +6)]: that is, Xan offers all the elements of a compensation but does not follow it through, so his additions remain nonconserving.

Dan (7;8), giving similar reactions to the same questions, classifies the parts according to similar size divisions and affirms equality by referring to the correspondence between elements and the singularity of the cut in each figure, $[(1)+(2+ \ . \ . \ . \ +6)]$ vs. $[(1+ \ . \ . \ . \ +4)+(5+6)]$. But when we add one cut to his figure, *that makes it bigger, longer on mine*. "But what about the whole string?" *Mine is longer*. "Can you arrange it so that it is the same?" *Yes, put it like that* [closing]. Later, he returns to this condition of *closing it all*.

The first progress of these subjects relative to those of level IA is that the cuts are no longer seen simply as creating discontinuities but as delimiting parts that vary in length. The result is that subjects constantly perform additions, depending on whether the elements are "put together" (Ovi) or separated; and these internal groupings are then classified as bigger or smaller, medium sized or small. This second progress raises a problem, which is the central question concerning associativity: how to explain that two wholes that must be equal to each other, since they are composed of equal elements, may contain parts of varying length (introduced by the cuts) when two figures are compared.

In fact, associativity can be compared to the *substitution* of classes: the same class formed of the same elements can be divided into subclasses in various ways, depending on the criteria used. In that case, the conservation of the whole does not present any problem, since these subclassifications are not quantitative and therefore do not require metric or numerical compensations. In contrast, associativity is a quantitative substitution so that any change in the parts requires compensation of increases in some parts by a corresponding decrease in the others. Xan seems to understand this, even explicitly, when he says that a cut "makes smaller [in one part] and bigger [in another]." But in spite of various intuitions of the same kind, these subjects still lack the ability to generalize to compensation. Even though subjects are unanimous in accepting the conservation of the whole by addition of its elements so long as one eliminates the cuts (when the whole is "closed," says Dan), the union of the parts does not equal the whole for these subjects. Addition, in this case, ceases to be conserving.

Level IIA

At 7-8 years of age, corresponding to the level of additivity involved in conserving length described in chapter 4, the subjects become capable of adding the parts as well as the elements—the two now being compatible. This establishes associativity in its logically necessary form. Let us first cite a few intermediate cases:

San (7;5), with six-element figures divided into $[(1)+)2+ \ . \ . \ . \ +6)]$ vs. $[(1+ \ . \ . \ . \ +4)+(5+6)]$ respectively: *Yes, it is the same because we've done the same cuts*. We widen the gap in the second figure. "It's more open now, but no string has been taken away?" *No*. "It's the same length?" *No, there is more string there.* "Why?" *I don't know.* "Show me the whole string." *No, we don't have the same. There* [(1)+(2+ . . . +6)], *there is more.* Then she changes her mind. We then propose [(1)+(2+3)+(4)+(5+6)] vs. [(1+ . . . +4)+ (5+6)]. *It's still the same. . . . Yours has more* [parts] *but they're smaller: mine has fewer, but they are bigger.* Thus, she gives evidence of comprehending compensation.

Sof (7;4) bases the equality of the whole upon that of the elements. When considering parts, Sof says: *I win because I have two pieces longer on my side.* But when presented with another grouping [(1)+(2+3)+(4)+(5+6)] as against [(1+ . . . +4)+(5+6)], *It's the same because before we had gates we had the same. The gates* [cuts], *that does not change anything.*

Pie (8;2), for the same question−[(1)+(2+ . . . +6)] and [(1+ . . . +4) +(5+6)]−says: *It's the same calculation but not the same length*[!]. *My side is much bigger here* [at the starting point] *than yours,* but *if you hook them up together, then it's the same length.* Toward the end, he achieves compensation: *Yours has more, the big end compared with my small one, and I take that* [1+2+3+4], *that is bigger than* [your] *small one. The two are the same.*

The obstacle encountered by these subjects is the lack of correspondence between "parts," which they then overcome by compensation. This finally leads to the establishment of the conservation of the whole. In the following subjects, conservation appears immediately or nearly so. Associativity is occasionally explicit.

Yve (6;10), after a moment's hesitation (with three elements): *Ah, it's the same: that* [1+2] *and that* [3] *make the same as that* [1] *and that* [2+3], *sure!"* Similarly, with four elements, she accepts immediately that [(1+2)+(3+4)] =[(1)+(2+3+4)].

Rim (7;0) simply invokes conservation: *We have the same, because we haven't taken any string away and because you have that* [(1)+(2+ . . . +6)] *and I have that* [(1+ . . . +4)+(5+6)].

Phi (7;4) similarly says, *We've only moved things, nothing taken away or added.* With four parts on one side and two on the other: "Isn't that strange?" *No.* "More pieces [parts] on yours?" *Yes.* "So there is more string?" *No.*

At this last level, the addition of the parts thus becomes just as natural as that of the elements: additivity has become conserving in the two cases. Subjects instantly understand the convergence of the two series, as they realize that the parts and their associations contain the same elements. The additive process has become inferential and is no longer subordinated to the observed perceptual data of the cuts. But before examining the question of what forms of necessity account for these advances, we shall have to look at situations in which associativity concerns not segments of an open linear structure, but initially closed figures transformed into open ones with or without fusions.

The Enclosure Task

The material consists of four 10-cm strings of different colors, which are built into patterns held together by pins.

Level IA

We observe here the reactions already known, those of *qualitative length* as determined by shape, orientation, and openness. Yet it seems useful to go back to these, since the results of the fence task sometimes create the impression of incomprehension rather than of instructive reactions.

Isa (4;5): "With this string [the four suspended, 1], we shall make a pattern [square]. Is it still the same size as before, [the string spread out]?" *It's smaller because it's square.* "Why smaller?" *Because there was no square before.* "And like that [a slight opening (a)]?" *A bit bigger because it's not really a square any more [(b)]. It's bigger because you've opened it more.* "What to do to make the string bigger?" He spontaneously draws (c). "But all that and all that [we follow the two paths]?" *Before it was bigger, it was like that* [straight line]. Somewhat later, a rectangle is bigger than a square *because it is a big square.*

Fre (4;10): We construct the three patterns of situation 3 for the child and the experimenter. Fre recognizes that the three make up the same path. We merge the first two into a large rectangle, leaving the third apart as is. The child keeps the three isolated ones: *You have the longest one.* "Why?" *Because there is that and that* [merged], *and I have three* [points to them]. We merge 1 and 2 on a square and do the same for the child's set, but using 2 and 3, leaving the remaining segment apart in both cases (3 for the adult, 1 for the child): *It's yours and mine* [i.e., correct recognition of the equality of the total paths]. After that, we build a square with 1 and 2 (3 apart) and a long triangle for the child with 2 and 3 (1 apart): *Mine is longer.* Then we build a variety of closed figures, each containing all three elements. Each time, the subject considers that there is inequality in favor of the more drawn-out forms. We go on to situation 1. Fre reacts like Isa vis-à-vis the open end. But when the oblique line is oriented inside the square, the path becomes shorter (on two temporally separate occasions).

Ria (4;7) believes that the square opened toward the outside makes the perimeter longer, one side oriented inside makes no difference, but two sides bent inside make it shorter.

Dan (5;8) has the same reactions with the opened squares. "To make it even longer?" *Put it all straight.* A cut producing an angle that scarcely modifies the orientation of the segment still makes it *longer, because we've cut it: now it's in pieces.* Situation 3: segments 1–2 made into a square+3 apart makes more than 1+2+3 *because you have a big line, you've mixed it.* "And to get the same length?" *I put 1 and 2 together and leave 3 as it is.*

Mic (5;7) thinks that a square and a triangle make *the same thing if you put them like this* [the two strings lengthwise], but if you keep the form, the triangle is longer because of the base. We change his square into variously shaped triangles. The longest is always the one with one side the longest. Situation 3: segments 1 and 2 made into a square with 3 apart, compared with 1 apart and 2+3 merged into a triangle, yield a judgment of the latter being longer because of the base.

Sca (5;8): A square with one side opened toward the inside is judged longer than the closed square but less long compared with a square with a side turned toward the exterior.

Tep (6;7) is worth citing because he seems to solve situation 3 spontaneously: a triangle (1+2) plus 3 apart will make *the same length* as 1 apart plus (2+3) united into a hexagon. "Why?" *We have two made into a big one and one little one.* (This may be the beginning of the compensations of level IB.) But (1+2) as a triangle is *longer* than (2+3) together, and 3 apart makes more than 1 alone because *it is a rectangle and it has a head.* In fact, there is no quantitative equality but only a single form of the whole in the two cases, and the apparent compensation is only figurate.

What is common between these reactions and those of the preceding section is the lack of additivity of elements or parts. In the case of situation 3, subjects do not compare (1+2)+3 with (1+2+3), which would be a form of associative addition in the wide sense. Instead, except for Tep, for the reasons we have just seen, they content themselves with judging the former combination as longer because it contains a "big line" (Ria). When the two first elements (1–2) and the two last elements (2–3) are combined but using different shapes, they deny equality. Thus, Fre judges the second set, a triangle, longer than the first, a square, because the base of the triangle is longer than that of the square.

When the combined part is identical on both sides, there is judged to be equality ("It's [the same in] yours and mine," says Fre); but the identity of forms is sufficient to explain these judgments, and it is not necessary to invoke addition of partial lengths.

As for the cuts, they have the same effect as seen for the subjects at this level in the earlier task. In both cases, they modify the total lengths. But a different reason applies in the present case: with a closed figure, a cut leads to a change in direction. In fact, if one side of a square is detached at one end, there are two possibilities: either it is oriented toward the exterior and there is an increase in length (see Isa's successive reactions to the variations shown in situation 1) or it is oriented toward the interior and the total length is judged diminished or unchanged (Fra and Dia). The comparisons between the pairs of closed figures confirm this decisive role of the lengthening of a side: it is sufficient for one side to be clearly longer than any other side in the comparison field for the child to conclude that there is more length involved. The overall size of the figure also clearly plays a part (as in Isa's "big square" for a rectangle). But it is not well differentiated from that of the perimeter or of the horizontal spread of the figure.

Levels IB and IIA

At level IB, we find the same conflicts as described for that level in the earlier task between emerging additivity with its first forms of compensations and factors determining inequalities, such as forms and orientations:

Tar (5;4) begins in situations 1 and 2 with level IA reactions, but when given situation 3 with (1+2) as a square and (+3) apart in one figure and (2+3) as a triangle and (1) apart in the other, Tar immediately furnishes a judgment of additive equality with compensation: *Because I have a big one* [2+3] *and a small one* [1] *and you have a big one* [1+2] *and a small one* [3]. "So, that makes the same length, if one takes the whole?" *Yes.* "Didn't you tell me that this triangle [2+3] is longer than this square [1+2]?" *Yes,* [so] *I have more than you.*

Gil (6;0) reasons at level IA in situation 1. In situation 2, Gil has to compare a triangle and a square made out of identical strings 10 cm long: "More or less?" *It's the same string. I've seen that the two were the same length.* "And now?" *No, no, we don't have the same length of string: a square, that makes more string than a triangle.* In contrast, in situation 3 with (1+2) and (3) as a triangle and (1+2+3) all separated: *This has more shapes, but it's the same length*; then, *No, you have more. . . . No, the two are the same. . . . If you put all of mine in that one* [the triangle], *one doesn't. . . . Yes, it's the same.*

Aur (6;2) is torn between the opposite extremes of the conflict. She begins situation 3 successfully: comparing (1+2)+3 with 1+2+3, she says that she has more length because she has not *put them together*, which gives her more pieces. But soon she corrects herself: *We've walked the same length* because the same elements, 1, 2, and 3, are found in the two different figures. But she regresses to inequality with a triangle and a hexagon because of 6>3 (sides).

Ago (6;4): In situation 1, the cuts change nothing concerning length: *You've only moved things around and it's the same.* Same success in situations 2 and 3: *That* [his 1], *I agree that it's much smaller than that* [1+2] *as a triangle; but I add that* [3 on the right] *and that* [at left] *and it comes out the same. I am smart!* But when he is asked whether the elements 1, 2, and 3 (form on both sides) have the same length, he first denies it, pointing to inequalities that turn out to be illusions upon verification with straight lines: *It's the same in size. You got me that time!* This shows that the conservation of the whole precedes that of the elements, even when the associative parts were added correctly: (1+2)+3= (1)+(2+3).

Sco (6;10) comes very close to associative additivity. In situation 3, with (1+2)+3=1+2+3, *We have both the same* [length] *because I could do the same thing* [figures] *as you.* He thus understands quantitative substitution (distributional change) in its principle, but he still thinks that *if you leave them* [the elements] *hooked up together, you have more, and if you undo them then it's not so much the same,* which amounts to just failing additivity.

Cat (7;1), in situation 1: *It's the same string, but not the same length,* up to the point where contradictions on 11 variations lead her to discover quantitative length. *It's the same length, but not the same design: yes, the string cannot get smaller and smaller or longer and longer. . . .* In situation 3, she concludes nevertheless that the total length is the same (parts and elements) *if you link them up. It's the same length, if you put them all together*; otherwise, *yours is longer, I only have small bits.* We have here a kind of material virtual addition made explicit by the subject, but not yet the inferential addition under conditions of separation of elements.

Gue (7;1) vacillates between one and the other. In situation 3, for $(1+2)+3=1+2+3$: *I have more. No, no, it's the same because those two* [the sum of $1+2$], *it's the same as that* [1 and 2 separate]. *If they're not together, you also have two.* Inversely, if one puts the separate ones together, one gets the same lengths of parts and wholes by adding up the parts and not just the elements: $(1+2)+(3)=(1)+(2+3)$. Still, he regresses again when comparing $(1+2+3)$ merged into a polygon with the set of separate figures 1, 2, 3.

Ani (7;8), like all the other subjects described here, remains nonconserving in responding to situation 1; but in situation 3 there is immediate success, by recourse to two arguments: *I can do like you* [with my components] *and it would be the same length*; and *We have the same strings.*

Fri (7;0) fails in situations 1 and 2; in 3, equality is first subordinated to the material union *if you put them together.* Then there is a breakthrough: *Because before, the strings were the same length: if you put them in a different order* (=different distribution, not serial order), *it will always be the same length.*

Let us cite two more cases of level IIA (7–8 years of age) before going on to the general discussion:

Jas (7;11), in situation 1: *Always the same length, but it's a different form.* Or, *It's the same, except here there's a piece that's cut. If you take it out* [of the figure], *then you have less, but* [if you leave it in] *it's the same* [in spite of the cut]. In situation 3, *The same length of string* and *I can fabricate* [your forms] *with my string.*

Pha (8;0), in situation 1: *Always the same, because you made* [at the start] *a square like mine.* In situation 3, *If I put these two forms together, it will make the same length as yours.*

At level IB, we discern progress in additivity. This progress manifests itself as follows: in comparisons (as with Tar, who does not stick to it, however) and in a particular form of virtual compensation or quantitative substitution, which consists in recognizing that one can modify one's forms and thus reproduce one's partner's shapes—that what is left separate could be "put together," and vice versa. But the strange thing about most of these level IB subjects is that even though they are quite proficient in imagining the possibility of these material additions and effective mergers, they continue to believe that only if they actually carry them out will there by equality, whereas without such a material realization the inequality persists. In level IIA subjects, the logical value of possible material additions is the same, whether they get actualized or not. This virtuality lends logical necessity to their concept of equality.

Another striking fact to be commented on with respect to level IB is that situations 1 and 2 are more difficult than that of associativity in progress (situation 3). It thus seems (and we shall return to this point) that the conservation of an isolated element whose form gets changed is less obvious than that of a whole of which parts get modified.

Conclusions

The first question we have to discuss with respect to the pro-structures, of which the associativity of lengths provides a simple example, concerns their status in relation to specific structures. At first glance, one might consider them structures of superior rank, since they include operations on operations: addition of elements to parts and of parts to wholes. But these wholes would be the same if they united only the elements without passing through the parts, and the latter result only from differentiations within the whole, like subclasses within a class and their possible variants (substitution classes). Thus, pro-structures are not to be confused with incomplete *pre-structures*; rather, they constitute the means by which structures are regulated. They serve among other things to ensure conservation under conditions of changes in form or distribution.

Before discussing the problem of necessities involved in associativity, let us resolve the problem already announced. Is it the conservation of elements that, when summed, brings about that of the whole? Does the process go in the opposite direction, or is the facilitation mutual? In many cases, subjects base their judgments of the equality of the two total lengths upon the invariance of their elements: "It's the same string," says Cat, "but not the same length." Thus, there is necessary conservation of the sum of the individual string segments. Or: "Before, the strings were the same length," and if you arrange them in some other way "it will always be the same length" (Fri). But two kinds of facts show independent conservation of the whole, with a possible effect on that of the elements, and a frequent lack of invariance of the elements taken in isolation. The whole as such presents two specific characteristics that facilitate its elementary conservation. First, there is compensation, by which the apparent additions and subtractions counteracting conservation are reduced to simple displacements: Ago reaches conservation of the whole in situation 3 (enclosure) but does not yet understand that it logically implies the conservation of the elements. The second fact is subjects' understanding that with the elements of a figurate whole, one can equally well construct the figure produced by the partner ("I can do like you," says Ani), which implies the invariance of elements.

But the most surprising fact of all is that many subjects are close to the conservation of the whole in situation 3 (enclosures) but remain quite far from it in situation 1. Thus, Ani (7;8), who performs successfully in situation 3, still believes that by slightly deviating one side of a square—barely separating it from the base—one increases length. A striking contrast appears here between the conservation of a complex whole in situation 3 and the lack of invariance of lengths within an elementary figure. This contrast appears in all subjects of level IB. Even though these subjects do not entirely master associativity, the mere opportunity of grouping the elements into parts variously distributed seems to facilitate conservation or at least an integration oriented in this direction. We thus conclude that conservation proceeds in both directions: from the elements to the whole and vice versa; that is, the two processes are in a relation of reciprocal implication.

But associativity cannot be reduced to only these two kinds of conservation, which are, however, necessary conditions; rather, its specific characteristic is the distribution of variable parts, which means quantitative substitution with compensations. In other words, it consists in differentiations with integrations such that the sum of the parts equals the whole as well as the sum of the elements. The problem posed by our research is that of the necessity inherent in conservation, not so much conservation of the parts as such (since these vary), but of their sum (which is equal to the sum of the whole and that of the elements). We shall try to account for this development as follows. In fact, it proceeds in the same way as any form of conservation. The latter is acquired when subjects understand that the differences between parts only result from the displacement of elements from one to another part and that the length to be evaluated has nothing to do with the changes in form but is determined only by the fact that the elements displaced conserve their proper length. In short, associativity results necessarily from conserving addition (=conserving the addends). Conversely, all conserving addition is necessarily associative because it conserves the sum of the parts, the differences between parts resulting only from the displacement of elements that are conserved in the process of changes in distribution.

As for the reasons explaining the conservation of length of displaced elements, they vary somewhat with the situation. In the case of commutability (enclosures, situation 3), they are to be seen in the necessary compensation between what is taken away at the starting point and what is added at arrival. In the case of simple connectability, they reside in the substitution of directions or positions, where what is conserved are adjacencies, which implies a relation of automorphism between the whole and the units, adjacent to each other, that compose it.

6

Multiplication and Multiplicative Associativity

with I. Berthoud-Papandropoulou and H. Kilcher

To analyze the associativity of additions in the preceding chapter, we did not need to begin with the study of the necessities proper to the constitution of addition itself, composition by union being a very primitive one. It was sufficient to refer to the decisive turning point, which is the transition from nonconserving addition, in which the addends are altered as a function of changes in form or position, to properly quantitative addition, requiring the conservation of the addends. But the conserving addition (as observed with level IIA) is not immediately always numerical or metrical. The latter development occurs only when the notion of unit is introduced.

The development of multiplication is much more complex. In principle, multiplication appears to be nothing more than addition of additions, but these are synthesized as a simultaneous composition instead of being carried out successively. Thus, $3 \times 4 = 12$ can be rewritten as $3 + 3 + 3 + 3 = 12$ or as $4 + 4 + 4 = 12$, where each addend contains in turn an internal addition, since $3 = 1 + 1 + 1$ and $4 = 1 + 1 + 1 + 1$. It is, however, easy to see the following difference. In the case of multiplication, one needs to distinguish three levels, analogous to those we have noted with respect to the associativity of addition. First, there is the *whole* (here 12, which remains identical under permutation, $3 \times 4 = 4 \times 3$); second, we have the subtotals, which we have called *parts* (we shall replace the term in this chapter by *containers* or *bundles*) — in our example, there are three classes each containing four elements; and third, there are the *elements* or units, here four in each of the parts, that play the role of *contained* in each of these parts. One might object that these distinctions can also be found in addition: for example, in $3 + 4 = 7$, 7 is the whole, 3 and 4 are the parts, and unities are the elements. But there is an important difference: in multiplication (this is particularly evident if multiplication is represented as addition of additions), the parts must be equal to each other, or contain the same number of elements. By contrast, in simple addition, determining the whole in no way requires equality between parts or even elements if, as was the case with the length segments in chapter 5, there are no metrical units to constitute. Thus, multiplication is much more complex and involves many more implicit quantifications. For this reason, it is of interest to study the stages of its development when it becomes differentiated from addition.

Method

Material: one toy sheep (*S*), one toy duck (*D*), one pile of identical grains.

Experimental situations: The same basic information is used in situations 1, 3, and 4. The sheep (*S*) eats three grains with each bite (=one bundle *S*) and the duck eats two (=one bundle *D*).

Situation 1, multiplication ($4 \times 3 = ? \times ?$). The experimenter prepares four bundles of three grains for *S*. Problem: prepare as many grains for *D*, respecting the basic information given above (*D* eats two grains with one bite).

Situation 2, associativity [$2 \times (4 \times 3) \overset{?}{=} (2 \times 4) \times 3$]. Basic information: *S* and *D* eat three grains per bite. The experimenter prepares two meals of four bundles each for *S*. Problem: prepare for *D* the same number of grains, but to be given at one meal. Variant: the experimenter again prepares two meals of four bundles each. The child is asked to prepare the same number of grains for *D*, also to be given in two meals. Once the collection is constituted, the child is asked about the equality of the two collections, *S* and *D*. Then the grains of *D* are placed in a pile. Problem: prepare for *D* the same amount to eat but in a single meal, using the grains from the pile.

Situation 3, commutative associativity ($2 \times 4 \times 3) = (3 \times ? \times 2$). The experimenter prepares two meals of four bundles each for *S*. Problem: prepare the same number of grains for *D* but in three meals, respecting the initial base information — three grains=one bundle *S*, two grains=one bundle *D*.

Situation 4, series of injective correspondences. The experimenter and the child simultaneously pick up a bundle *S* (=three grains) and a bundle *D* (=two grains), respectively. This activity is repeated six times. After that, the two collections are hidden. Problem: decide whether the two collections contain the same number of grains. Evaluate the numerical difference between the two collections. Generalize this evaluation to a large number *n* of repetitions of the same activity (=prediction).

Each situation involves the following variables of three different rank levels characteristic of multiplication that we identified above:

Elements = number of grains per bundle
Parts   = number of bundles
Whole   = number of grains (total).

These variables correspond to the terms *multiplicand*, *multiplier*, and *product* used in traditional descriptions of multiplication: number of bundles × number of grains per bundle=the total (whole). Situations 2 and 3 (which deal with associativity) also introduce a supplementary variable—the number of meals—that corresponds to another multiplier and relativizes the status of the variable *number of bundles*, which thus changes from that of multiplier to that of multiplicand in a new composition: number of meals × number of bundles × number of grains / bundle=total number of grains.

The developmental interest of the study is to establish for each age level the status that children attribute to each of the variables and how they compose them (simultaneously or not, etc.) to solve the problems proposed. But our main objective is to discover the bases of the reasons (whether made explicit or not) that underlie these compositions and that are the foundations for the judgments and the constructions of equalities and inequalities. Our experimental situations were not conceived only to provoke judgments from the children—for example, $2 \times (4 \times 3) = (2 \times 4) \times 3$; nevertheless, judgments are solicited about the constructions produced by the child (about a collection that is considered equal to a standard collection); such judgments will be analyzed in the light of the constructions accompanying them.

Level IA

Subjects at this level are able to focus on each of the variables distinguished above, but they manipulate only one variable at a time and ignore ones that they manipulated before when they go on to the next. This has two consequences: the first is a lack of coordination between contained and container variables; therefore there are also no compensations that would follow from each consideration of the changes in the interrelations between variables. The second consequence is little coherence and much contradiction in subjects' responses, to which they are entirely insensitive.

Cri (4;11), in situation 1 ($S=4$ parts of 3; D requires 2 g per bite:* she gives 4 parts of 3 g to D, the same as S. "Do you remember? He takes bites of two." She then makes 4 p of 2 g. "Do they both have the same amount to eat?" *Yes.* We simplify by giving S only 2 p of 3 g. Cri then makes 4 p of 2 g for D. "Is it the same amount?" *Ah, no!* She corrects to 2 p of 2 g. In situation 2, S gets 4 p of 3 g in the morning and in the evening and D has to eat as many g in a single meal: Cri packs 4 p of 3 g. "Do they eat the same amount?" *Only the sheep eats four.* "Four of what?" *Four grains in the morning and four grains in the evening* [thus she confuses p and g]. "So how many parts do we have to give to the duck?" *Four.* "Do they eat the same amount?" *Yes.* "One does not have more?"

---

*Let us recall the abbreviations: S=sheep, D=duck, p=parts or bundles, g=grains, and e=elements.

Yes, the sheep has more. "It can be fixed up?" *No, because the sheep eats four in the morning and in the evening four more.* Then we prepare for *D*, as for *S*, 4 *p* of 3 *g* and also less than that; then we mix up in a pile the *g* belonging to *D*, asking the child to make one single meal from it. She prepares 4 *p* of 3 *g* and discards the rest: *There.* "What about all the rest?" *He doesn't eat that.* "Why?" *He has to eat the same as the sheep.* "And is that the same?" *Yes, because here* [*D*] *it's four, here* [*S*, morning] *it's four also and four* [evening]. Her interpretation of 4 is thus qualitative (intensional) and not numerical (extensional). At last we ask her to compare 2 (meals)×4 (*p*)×3 (*g*) with 8 (*p*)×3 (*g*). *The duck has more, because he has all that* [8×3].

Phi (5;5), for 4 *p* of 3 *g* to *S*, gives 3 *p* of 2 *g* to *D*. "How much did you give to the duck?" *Two* [confuses *p* and *g*]. "Do they eat the same amount?" *No* [she adds one *p* of 3 *g* for *D*]. "That makes the same amount?" *Yes* [she points to all of *D*'s]. We simplify: 2 *p* of 3 *g* for *S*: she puts down 2 *p* of 2 *g* for *D*. "Like that, it's the same?" *Yes.* "Could you show how?" *It's the sheep who has more* [points to the whole]. "What to do?" She puts down 2 *p* of 3 *g* in *D*'s place and in *S*'s, forgetting the instruction 2 by 2.

Cla (5;11), for 4 *p* of 3 *g* to *S*, puts down 4 *p* of 2 *g* for *D*. "Do they eat the same amount?" *No.* "So?" he corrects to 4 *p* of 3 *g* for *D*. "But he takes bites of two!" *Two bundles of two grains* [to *D*]. We build him a pile of 6 in disorder, corresponding to 3×2 for *S* and the same for *D*. He takes 2 away from *D* and ends up once more with 2 *p* of 3 *g* for *S* and 2 *p* of 2 *g* for *D*.

Isa (6;7), in situation 1: for 4 *p* of 3 *g* to *S*, she gives 4 *p* of 2 *g* to *D*. "Do they have the same?" *No, the sheep has more: he eats a bunch divided in two* [2 and 1 *g*]. "Put these grains by twos here and I'll put mine in threes there." This is done four times with 3 on one pile and 2 *g* on the other. "We have the same or not?" *I think so, because we started at the same time and stopped at the same time, we have the same.* Situation 2: for two meals of 4 *p* of 3 *g* to *S*, Isa only gives 4 *p* of 2 *g* to *D*. "They eat the same amount?" *The sheep has a little bit more.* We prepare two sets of 2×(4 *p* of 3 *g*) each, mix up the second, and ask Isa to start over with *p* of 3: she puts up 4 *p* of 3. *Is that alright?* "Do you think it's the same amount?" *Yes* [hesitates]. "What is to be done?" She adds a fifth *p* of 3 *g*, then a sixth one, after which she declares equality.

These facts are of obvious significance for arriving at an understanding of how multiplication is constructed. We see immediately that the compositions that would be necessary for multiplicative solutions are deficient. In fact, even the simplest multiplications are not yet realized.

In general, the preceding reactions are characterized by the incomprehension of the necessary inclusion relation between the three hierarchically ordered systems. We distinguished the elements or grains, the parts or bundles, and the whole itself that has to be conserved. Subjects cannot see the impossibility of determining the totals and their equalities solely on the basis of the number of bundles without taking into account the number of grains that they contain. Actually, the bundles, even though contained in the whole, play the part of *containers* with respect to the grains that they comprise and that constitute the *contained* within the bundles, which only then become the contained with respect to the whole. As we have already seen in chapter 5 when we dealt with associativity in the addition of length, what poses a problem at this initial level is the dual nature of the situation—that is, the fact that the parts are simultaneously contained in the whole and contain the elements. This explains the tendency, at first practically invincible, to consider only one of these relationships at any one time.

The first reaction of each of these subjects is to give D 4 parts of 2 grains since S has 4 parts of 3 grains and D has to eat in bites of 2. The lack of differentiation goes so far as to make subjects like Cri and Phi at a given moment confuse bundles and grains (according to Cri, S eats 4 grains in the morning and in the evening, whereas he actually eats 4 bundles of 3 grains each). With respect to associativity, while S receives 2 meals of 4 bundles of 3 grains, subjects often give D only a single set of 4 bundles of 3 grains, as if the equality of the wholes depended only on the qualitative distribution (4 bundles of 3 g). When Cri is given the same number of grains S has (24) to distribute to D in an unordered pile, and when asked to arrange them in triplets, he correctly constructs 8 bundles of 3 g but considers this far too many to achieve equality. This judgment results from thinking only of the number of bundles.

When the subjects notice that there is no longer equality (only in the overall configurations), they attempt to find a solution by local actions on the number of grains per bundle (1 more for S than for D) or on the number of meals. They finally come to the conclusion that a solution is impossible or that it consists in identical distributions (4 parts of 3 grains to each animal). This, of course, is not a real solution. It is based on a restrictive principle according to which wholes can be equal only if all their components are. This view lacks any comprehension of the necessarily hierarchical way in which the three systems are nested one inside the other. In such a structure, the parts have a dual function: as contained within the whole and containers in relation to the grains.

Level IB

Reactions at this level consist in attempts to establish relations between the variables. In particular, subjects begin to relate the parts p to the grains g in terms of container and contained. Hence we observe certain correct solutions, even though the problem of compensation is not entirely solved in this situation. Let us first cite two intermediate cases between levels IA and IB:

Dia (5;0), in situation 1: for $S=4$ p of 3 g, she gives 4 p of 2 g to D. *There!* "That's the same number of grains?" *Yes.* "You see that?" *By looking at three.*

"Count them." *Three, three, three, and three.* "And the duck?" *Two.* "And the sheep, how many little piles does he have?" She counts the contents of a *p*. *Three.* "And the duck, how many piles has he? *Four also.* "And who has the most grains?" *The sheep.* "What is to be done?" *Add a third* [i.e., 4×3 as for *S*]. "But he eats two at a time." She adds 2 *p* of 2 *g*, which is correct, but she feels obligated to add 1 *p* of 2 *g* to *S*. *Like that, they both have the same.* "And what if you take that away [the additional (*p*×2 *g* of *S*]?" *No, because otherwise they do not have the same.* "And that too [1 *p* of 2 *g* to *S*]? And that also [another *p* of 2 *g*?" *No.* Situation 2: *S* receives 4 *p* of 3 *g* two times. "And the duck?" She puts down *p* of 3, 10×3, 12×3, up to 16×3. "They eat the same?" *The duck eats more.* "So?" She takes everything away except 2 times 4 *p* of 3 *g*, as for one of *S*'s meals. "It's the same now?" *Yes.* We add 2 *p* of 3 *g* to *D*. "One eats more?" *The duck.* We present 2 times 4 *p* of 3 *g* for *S* and the same for *D*, then we arrange the latter in a pile: "Can you arrange that?" She manages 8 *p* of 3 *g* empirically. The solution is correct, but she finds that this makes more for *D*. So she reduces it to 7 *p* of 3 *g*. *Now, I've made them the same.*

Sop (5;7) begins as at level IA: 4 *p* of 3 *g* to *S* and 4 *p* of 2 *g* to *D*. "Is that the same?" *No, the sheep eats by threes and the duck by twos.* "What to do?" She takes one away and adds some grains to each *p* of *S* and of *D*: thus, 4 *p* of 3 *g* for each. "But he eats by twos?" She manages 6 *p* of 2 *g* for *D*, but unordered and without noticing that she has achieved equality. She arranges four rows of 2 with four lines of 1 interspaced: *S* eats 2+1 and *D* eats the 2 only. This gives 4 *p* of 3 and 4 *p* of 2, her initial solution.

The following are clear cases:

Mur (6;7): *S*=4 *p* of 3. She gives *D* 4 *p* of 2 but then stops, counts the grains, and concludes that *S* eats more: *I shall add one bundle* [hence 5 *p* of 2]. We start over: *I look at the sheep, I count the grains. I look here* [D], *the same value.* She ends up with 6 *p* of 2: *I copied from the sheep to give to the duck. I gave a lot more bundles to the duck..*

Rob (6;5), for 4 *p* of 3 *g*, gives 4 *p* of 2. *Oh, no!* He makes correspondence between the 4 *p* of 3 and the *p* of 2, saying: *Another one* [5 *p* of 2]. "They eat the same?" *No, the sheep eats more, we just have to add two small ones for the duck.* But he is in no way convinced and transforms the 4 *p* of 3 into 6 *p* of 2 to be sure. He even concludes that *one has to count to be sure.*

Yva (6;10), for 4 *p* of 3, gives 4 *p* of 2. "They have the same?" *No.* She adds up to 8 *p* of 2 and finally corrects this to 6 *p* of 2, after having counted 12 and 12.

Luc (6;6), in situation 1: for the two meals of *S*, Luc immediately gives 7 *p* of 2 to *D*, except that *S* has more with two meals. But to be sure, *one has to count the grains of the sheep—if there are more here* [D], *we'll take some away.* "And if there isn't enough after that?" *Then I'll put some back.*

The intermediate case of Dia is interesting because she begins with level IA reactions but then comes to understand that by adding parts of 2 *g* for *D*, one can equalize the grains between S and D. But since she is still convinced that one also has to equalize the bundles, she adds inappropriately to S. Sop, likewise, begins with level IA reactions, realizes the problem, and tries to vary both p and g. But having arranged 6 p of 2 g for D, she does not realize that she has found the correct solution. So she builds a contrived arrangement, where S eats by threes and D by twos plus the leftover units.

As for the clear cases, there are two main novelties that the subjects come to discover: that the bundles or parts constitute *containers*, comprising the grains as *contained* elements; and that by adding bundles of two grains for D one obtains, as Mur says with some surprise, "a lot more bundles for the duck" while trying to "copy" from S.

The new relation of contained to container is not explicit, but it is clearly revealed in the following observations. After having counted the grains to check for equality following the first trial, subjects never add or take away isolated grains to or from already constructed bundles. Rather, they give D more bundles of two. As for the compensation wherein the fewer grains per bundle→the greater the number of bundles, this is far from being anticipated as a general relation yet it gets recognized a posteriori when subjects analyze their initial mistakes to find the reasons, which they are quick to find. However, anticipation is still a long way off, as we can see when Rob, Yva, and Luc declare that "one has to count" to be sure, even in the case of a correct prediction (by chance) ("We just have to add two small ones for the duck.").

Level IIA

At 7–8 years of age, several new developments have to be noted. The first is the stabilization of the three hierarchical systems of the whole, the parts or bundles, and the elements or grains: the bundles are, in particular, readily understood as being contained in the whole and as containers for the grains, whose number is constant for the p of S and D but not between the two "because one eats in small portions and the other in big ones," as Ana says. The second essential novelty is that the whole is no longer given only as the total number of grains, but appears as conserved when the relation of contained to container gets modified. Thus, this relationship develops toward a multiplicative relation. The third development is that, since the containers are modifiable and can be decomposed, the contained elements can be redistributed into new containers. This enables subjects to regroup the bundles and grains of S according to the distribution in pairs required for D: each grain 3 that is in excess in S becomes an element constituting another p of 2 for D. Such behavior is frequent at this level, constituting a test in action of the hypothesized relation np of $xg = n'p$ of yg, where the child demonstrates the substitution by which one can go from one distribution to another. This is, in fact, another example of *quantitative substitu-*

tion, as in the case of associativity of length additions. Finally, the fourth development: the quantitative nature of these substitutions implies compensations such that if $n>n'$, then $x<y$ (or if $n<n'$, then $x>y$).

Cor (7;7), in situation 1: 4 p of 3 g for S. She immediately counts $3+3=6$, $6+6=12$, and when reminded that D eats in bites of two, she immediately puts up 6 p of 2 g for D. "the little kids say that that one [D] has six bundles and that one there [S] four." *Because there are bundles of three and bundles of two.* Situation 3: she counts 24 for three meals of S and proposes 5 p of two for D's breakfast and 7×2 for his supper, which comes out alright as 24, but not as two halves.

Ana (7;0): For 4 p of 3 g given to S, she puts up 4 p of 2 g and adds 2 p of 2g for D. "Why?" *I gave four bundles for the bundle of the sheep, and there* [third element of each p of S] *I took one by one and I made little piles* [2 p of 2 g to put to D's account]. For 2 p of 3 g to S, she gives 3 p of 2 g to D; and for 3 p of 3 g to S she sees that it takes 4 p of 2 g with 1 in excess, *otherwise there is always one* [that stays] *alone.* "But why is it that here the two have 12 and there the duck has six bundles and the sheep four?" *Because one eats in small portions and the other in big ones.* For situation 3, she solves the problem by transforming the configuration of D into that of S, hence $3\times(4\times2)=2\times(4\times3)$: "But as bundles, it's very different?" *Yes, but they still have the same number of grains.*

Dom (7;1), in situation 1, gives 4 p of 2 g to $D+3$ more, which gives 1 too many. She checks S's configuration by taking away the third grain of each p. This tells her that there are 6 p of 2 g (for D) corresponding to S's 4 p of 3 g. Situation 3: she distributes S's two meals as 4 p of 3 g; then, without counting, she lines up two rows of grains in such a way that to each possible pair for S there corresponds 1 p of 2 g—i.e., 12 p of 2 g. Then she redistributes them as 3×4 p of 2 g by simple correspondence, without numerical calculation.

Dam (8;3) constructs his 6 p of 2 g for D by correspondence with the last (third) of the $2+1$ g of each of S's piles. His general explanation is *because in three there is two.*

Bea (8;11) says that S has fewer p *because there are more in his bundles*. Situations 2 and 3 are solved by correspondence with the grains S has in excess in each bundle, at two meals, *because one can count two by two there and three by three there; it always comes out as 24.*

At level IIA, where subjects begin to understand the inclusion relations involved, we have to see whether the concepts used by the subjects implicate multiplicative actions or simple additions. The aim of genetic epistemology is not to explain the psychogenesis of knowledge with reference to the history of the sciences, but rather the opposite, so far as this is possible. Whatever our terminology, we are interested here in what the subject does rather than the analogies or differences between the subject's behaviors and what mathematicians today call addition and multiplication.

The central fact that dominates all subjects' reactions is that the bundles or parts are understood as *containers* and their grains or elements as *contained* — irrespective of the particular task dealt with, whether constructing 6 p of 2 g to correspond to the given 4 p of 3 g or establishing a correspondence by mentally rearranging the S's p of 3 g to create a new distribution with p of 2 g for D. Subjects seek to modify not the individual elements (except to reconstitute the bundles of 2 g) but rather the bundles as such with their predetermined number of grains. And when a subject has attained understanding of the fundamental equivalence $n(p \text{ of } xg) = n'(p \text{ of } yg)$ (generally also comprehending the internal relationship: if $n < n'$, then $x > y$), this certitude suffices to ensure the conservation of the whole, with or without supplementary arguments.

When we compare this situation with, among others, that of the addition of length, we note that the trilogy of whole, parts, and elements only appears in the problems involving associativity; however, in a simple addition like $4 + 3 = 7$, the addends 4 and 3 are not containers in the sense used here. There are two reasons for that: first, the addends only contain unities and are only a shorthand notation for $(1, 1, 1, 1) = 4$. In this expression, these unities do not figure as elementary addends (this would only be true of a series $n \rightarrow n + 1$, which is constitutive in the construction of integers but does not apply to additions in general; in the expression $4 + 3 = 7$, the term 3 is in no way thought of as being contained in 4, since in this particular case it is added from the outside). In comparing an addition like $4 + 3 = 7$ to the multiplication $4 \times 3 = 12$, the important difference is thus that the addend 4 is of the same rank as 3 and only contains unities. In contrast, $4 \times 3 = 12$ means that the union of unities comprised in the contained (= future multiplicand) 3 is to be taken 4 times because these containers (= future multipliers) are of a different rank, indicating the number of containers or bundles to unite to obtain the intended product. These four containers or bundles do not constitute, nor do they contain, unities in the same sense as does the addend 4, since they refer to certain well-determined numbers for any given distribution.

Second, the result of the fact just cited is that addends cannot be used as repeatable units, as can the parts with respect to the whole: even in a series of addends like $4 + 3 + 6$, etc., there is only one 4, and if several were to be used — as in the 4 parts of 3 g for S and the 6 parts of 2 g for D — one would have to write 4 (1 of 3) and 6 (1 of 2). At this point, even if the subject proceeds by addition to find the correct number of grains and does not give $4 \times 3 = 2 \times 6$, the bundles (parts, containers) she constructs and uses in actions are not simple addends because there are several of the same type, each with its particular contained elements. The expression "n containers of $x = ?$" can only have a multiplicative sense, even if the subject does not know her multiplication table. To reserve this latter term only for numerical multiplication would be to adopt a rather nondevelopmental perspective, linking it too strongly to school learning. Yet its development is highly instructive in that at level IIA there is strong emphasis on the relationship of contained-container, but the latter is not deployed in the case of additive "addends."

Another argument in favor of multiplications in action is that sometimes subjects engage in regrouping activities that can in no way be considered subtractions, but rather are functional equivalents of division even though they proceed by correspondence! Thus, Dom regroups $2 \times (4\ p$ of $3\ g)$ as $3 \times (4\ p$ of $2\ g)$ to correspond to three meals for D.

The strategy most frequently used at this level is what we call *quantitative substitution*. It consists in transforming the S-distribution into one required for D by pairwise projecting onto D the four elements that S's bundles have in excess so that their initial $4\ p$ of $2\ g$ are completed by two new p of $2\ g$. This strategy raises two distinct problems. First, this projective procedure is essentially additive because it concerns only the elements (grains), ensuring their equality in the two sets S and D. But it does not permit prediction of the number of bundles it will yield (in fact, these are never anticipated by subjects at this level because, in general, they make no predictions, in contradistinction to level IIB subjects). Second, this total number is arrived at by an empirical search. Still, it is remarkable (and this constitutes the truly multiplicative acquisition of this level) that subjects, having understood the relation between contained and containing, are quite certain that the new distribution (by 2) will allow them to specify the new containers and that the union of these new containers will comprise the same number of elements as those of S.

Thus, it would be a strong underestimation to consider the strategies used by the level IIA subjects as purely additive. We have to distinguish carefully the procedures used before any kind of anticipation and the final comprehension of results obtained by trial and error. Of course, it is not surprising that these remain additive up to the point where the equality between the products of the two distributions is noted, given the lack of the operational instruments of multiplicative anticipation. But what is really important is the interpretation of the results obtained. When subjects spontaneously realize that six containers of two elements give the same product as four containers of three elements, this is clearly comprehension of inclusion relations that go beyond simple summations. Although when Dom arranges her total in three parts $-3 \times 8\ p$ of $2\ g$ $-$ she may not know anything about division as an operation and may proceed by correspondence only, the outcome is nevertheless a distributed product. In short, what is missing at this level is the kind of anticipation that would translate *containers* into *multipliers* and *contained* into *multiplicands*. Yet subjects treat these problems in terms of distributions, nested relations, and number of containing and contained elements, specifying the numbers necessary for each. It would be difficult not to see in these behaviors multiplications in action preceding numeral schematization, parallel to similar sequences in all other domains, where concepts in their finished form evolve from organized actions.

This accomplishment occurs at the same level (II) where subjects come to deal adequately with the associativity of lengths, even though the latter acquisition seems a great deal simpler. In principle, it only involves the equality $(A+B)+C=A+(B+C)$. But, as we saw in chapter 5, subjects have difficulty in comprehending that variable parts are included within an invariant whole formed of identical elements, and this seems to interfere with the invariance of the whole. The same problem presents itself again in the case of multiplication; but an additional complication appears that may seem considerable: not only are the parts or bundles variable in number depending on how they are distributed to exhaust the entire set, but the contained elements are also variable and inversely related to the number of parts. This is all the more revealing in that it shows that the comprehension of the basic relation of containing→contained enables subjects to overcome these additional complications of multiplication. To be sure, this is achieved only by trial and error and successive readings rather than by anticipation, as will be the case at the following level.

Levels IIB (9–10 years) and III (11–12 years)

It is difficult to specify the developmental relationship between level IIA, where one hardly perceives any influence of school knowledge, and the following, IIB, where children have learned that $3\times4=12$, $2\times6=12$, and so on. But knowing the difficulties of assimilating school knowledge without the prerequisite, spontaneously acquired schemata, we cannot believe that all that is needed to convert containers into multipliers, contained elements into multiplicands (i.e., to transform a supposedly additive into a multiplicative relation), is to attach numbers to these entities. Let us further recall that the surplus procedure transferring the third term of each of the (4×3) bundles to the D set does not determine the number of containers, but only verifies the equality of the total contained elements. The essential difference between levels IIA and IIB, therefore, is that at IIA subjects proceed by empirical search regarding the containers, whereas at IIB they tend to anticipate. However, although they certainly make use of acquired methods of computation (in school or spontaneously), these are nevertheless guided by a logical necessity already discovered at level IIA: that a whole can be divided into different containers and that there is an inverse relationship between their number and that of the contained elements. Herein lies the foundation of the multiplicative relation, which is only extended and made more precise by anticipated numbering (numeration) (in the same way, numerical addition appears later than addition without units and anticipation).

Dan (9;7), with S having 4 p of 3 g, promptly lays down 6 p of 2 g for D:

I said to myself that 4 times 3 makes 12 and 6 times 2 makes 12. But, in situation 3 she hesitates as at level IIA. She first does not know how to handle *S*: two meals; then finally she finds $2 \times 12 = 24$ and attempts to arrange this into three meals for *D*, finding that 4 *p* of $2 = 8$ *p* of 2 is not enough for three meals. At last, she discovers: *I said to myself that 24, that is 3 times 8.*

Cat (9;5), in situation 1: *I shall put . . . six bundles of two.* "How did you do that?" *I've done it like that* [indicates bijections between *S* and *D*] *in my head.* Situation 3: $S = 4$ *p* of 3 *g*, morning and evening. He calculates a total of 24 for *S*; but when translating *S*'s 4 *p* of 3 *g* into 6 *p* of 2 *g* of *D*, he confuses grains and bundles for a moment and ends up with inequalities, to which his final comment is: *No, he has 24, I made a mistake.*

Lau (9;7), in situation 1: *I thought there [S], there are three [g], and then I counted $3 + 3 = 6$, 9. 12. So, one has to put the same amount here [D], but in pairs — four bundles of two grains and another two bundles — so it's complete.* We hide *D*. "Do you think that there are 12 there too?" *Yes, four bundles here* [as for *S*] *and two there* [thus, a correspondence of part to part]. Situation 3: he counts the grains of one meal for *S* as 12, then for two meals, and obtains $2 \times 12 = 24$. But for the three meals of *D*, he tries to calculate by *times*; and since there are three rations, he arranges 3×3, *no*, $3 \times 6 = 18$. "Is that correct for the duck?" *No, I've counted wrong, I should have done it by "plus": $2 + 2 + 2$ . . . ,* but he still ends up with 18. *I'll try like that: it makes 8 in the morning, 10, 12, 14, 16 here* [noon] *and 18, 20, 22, 24 here* [evening]. *That's right.* "Is there a way to find 24 right away?" *No, one has to try "times" first and then "plus."*

Oli (9;5), in situation 1: *The same thing, counting 2 by 2. For example, if the sheep takes 6, the duck takes 6 like that: 00 . . 00 . . 00.* Situation 3: *S* will eat 2 (meals) $\times 4$ [$n \times 3(g)$], which he distributes in twelves, and 12 *p* of 2. To prepare *D*'s meals, he divides the grains into 4 groups of 2 per meal: *I do it in my head: in the morning the sheep has 12 grains, and in the evening, too — a total of 24 grains. To arrange the duck's I took away from the sheep 1, 1, 1, 1. Then I separate the rest in 4 pairs per meal, so: $3 \times 8 = 24$.* "And the sheep?" *It's 2×12 grains.*

To compare levels IIB and IIA better, let us first examine level III, where a new strategy appears. Starting out with the whole, which is conserved, the subjects proceed to partition it into unequal distributions in such a way that the product of parts or bundles by grains remains constant:

Yva (10;10), in situation 1: *I gave it out so that there would be the same everywhere: there [S], there are 12 in all, I have to do 6×2. The sheep had 12, which was 3×4, and the duck, there are also 12: 2, that makes $6 \times 2 = 12$.* Situation 2: *There [S] are 12 and 12, a total of 24. There, too [D], the morning, that makes 8, the afternoon 8, and the evening 8. So that makes 24.*

Hen (10;1), in situation 1: *I look at the sheep's and transform them into bundles of 2: that makes bundles.* Situation 3: *I'll take the sheep's and the duck's, count them both up, and divide them by 3. I divide it into three meals* [although he was not instructed to divide by 3]. *Yes, it works, it's the same number; it comes to 24.*

Did (10;5) immediately distributes D's 12 into 6 p. Situation 3: He quickly discovers that it takes 4 bundles per meal, hence 24 divided by 2 for S and by 3 for D. *Twenty-four for each, 12 + 12 for the sheep and 8 + 8 + 8 for the duck.* "So that makes what?" *Eight bundles per meal . . . 8 grains, 24 grains per meal.* "Which is right? You divided by 3?" *Because he eats three times a day.* "So, what do you find?" *Eight grains* [hesitates]. "In what?" *Per meal.* "So how many bundles?" *Three, no 4* [he does 4 bundles of 2]. "And how many times are you going to do that?" *Three times.* "And that gives you 24?" *Yes* [sure].

Dan (11;3) immediately distributes 6 p of 2 g for D, corresponding to $3 \times 4 = 12$ for S. Situation 3: *It's $24 \div 3$, $3 \times 8 = 24$; so, the duck, at three meals a day, eats 8 bundles of 2 grains . . . 2 grains, 8 bundles: I have a few problems. . . .* "What are 3 and 8?" *The 24, the total number of grains.* "And the 3?" *The meals.* "And the 8?" *That's the number I used to arrive at 24*[!]. "And that's what?" *All of the grains he eats at one meal: 3 times a day and 4 bundles* [of 2].

Sto (12;0), in situation 3: *That makes 24 there* [S]. *Here $24 \div 3 = 8$ bundles.* "How many bundles per meal, for the duck?" *Eight bundles.* "How did you get that?" *For the grains, it makes $24 \div 3 = 8$. No. I made an error. It makes 8 grains per meal and 4 bundles in one meal.*

These subjects, whom one might call level IIIA, although having good control of the elementary numerical multiplications, still flounder in situation 2 because when D has more meals, he should have fewer p per meal. But when eating only two meals, he would have more p with fewer g per p. In other words, these subjects still have problems with the dual nature of the bundles, the fact that they are both contained and containing. At level IIIB, however, this difficulty is eliminated almost immediately:

Lyd (12;10): *The sheep has 8 bundles: $8 \times 3 = 24$. The duck will have 4 per meal. We thus have to divide 24 by 3 and by 2, because instead of eating 3 he only eats 2 at one bite, so 24 grains: $3 \times (8 \div 2 = 4)$.* She draws two sets of four and understands that she should say *4 bundles of 2 grains. The $8 \div 2$ has mixed me up.*

Reactions at levels IIB, and even at IIIA, reveal the same phenomenon that strikes one in all the research on multiplication: subjects have little difficulty with the computations involved but encounter problems with their meaning in particular applications. The typical example here is the problem subjects have with the meaning of 8 in the operation $24 = 3 \times 8$ (since the total is 24 and D eats these in three meals). But what does 8 represent? Dan, who is 11 years old, first says prudently: "That's the number I used to arrive at 24." Only somewhat later does he succeed in giving a concrete interpretation in terms of containers (grains per meal) and therefore of their contained elements: 4 bundles of 2 g. This is not surprising in view of the fact that the experimental situations involving associativity are complicated because the hierarchy comprises not only the three systems (the whole, the parts or bundles, and the elements or grains), but an additional container (the number of meals, contained in the whole but containing with respect to the bundles, which, in turn, are containing with respect to the grains). This makes it more difficult for subjects to remember, in the course of their numerical operations, what each number stands for within the system of containing-contained, which has evolved into one of mutliplier-multiplicand.

These facts lead us to propose a distinction between addition and multiplication that is richer than that used by our subject Lau, the system with which we had been content to work until now: to calculate a whole from n of its equal parts, p, one could proceed, like Lau, by a calculation in terms of "times"—i.e., $n \times p = T$—or by one in terms of "plus": $p + p + p$ . . . T. In this case, multiplication would only be an addition of additions. Its specificity would then consist only in constructing a thematic of the number of times, n, that the addition is to be performed—i.e., $T = np$. But the facts presented above suggest that the multiplicative system comprises two further requirements. It involves three-level hierarchies (as opposed to additions, which are not nested but only imply linear sequences): the contained, or basic elements, nested within the parts (or bundles, etc.) that serve as containers; and, finally, the whole as the union of all parts, which represent contained elements with respect to it. Thus, psychologically, the notions of multiplicand and multiplier represent the contained and containing terms of the system. That is, in the expression $4 \times 3 = 12$, the multiplicand 3 is contained in each of the 4 multipliers (a relationship that does not hold for addends, which are all of the same rank except in the case of associativity, but even there in a much less systematic form). The second requirement involved in multiplicative systems is just as essential and even more productive. It is the possibility for a whole to vary in terms of elements (e), by parts (p), and by their number—the possibility of changing the distribution of parts vs. elements within the whole by formalizing the relation between these different distributions, as follows: $T = n(p$ of $xe) = n'(p'$ of $ye)$ or $n' > n$ if $y < x$. The multiplicative system is thus much more flexible and richer than are additive systems.

Therefore, it is of interest to describe the stages in its construction. We have seen that this development begins with the comprehension of the relation between container and contained, which is already present at level IIA, even though these subjects do not anticipate results but only construct them step by step in empirical fashion. In this respect, the *surplus* method (reducing the 3 p of S to $2 + 1g$ and regrouping the leftover 1 g into p of 2 g) is a marvelous example of the equivalence of the products of these distinct distributions. What counts is not the procedure in its detail, but the subjects' conviction that two distributions like 4 p of 3 e and 6 p of 2 e are equivalent, where the pairwise projections only assure that none of the elements e are forgotten and that their total number remains the same. At the next levels (IIB and IIIA), the numerical anticipations increase but are accompanied by a new, troublesome factor: as the number of variables to be computed increases, the subjects' ability to group into a simultaneous whole—their concrete meanings and their inclusion relations—diminishes.

Conclusions

The development of necessity from one level to the next is a good example of continuity within a system of what may appear to be transformations of considerable magnitude. At level IA, the only relation that seems necessary is that subordinating the whole to the number of parts or bundles, without regard to their contained elements. As usual, we can see here both pseudonecessity (=error to be corrected) and prenecessity (the factor in question will be retained and completed at later levels). Subjects discover some of these factors themselves, but as yet without composition. Authentic necessities, however, cannot develop in the absence of such compositions.

At level IB, subjects begin to work out the relations between the number of bundles and that of their contained grains. But this remains in a state of prenecessity in the sense that it is a good direction to take but is not accompanied by success in detail (particularly compensations). But at level IIA, four kinds of necessity come to be recognized: (1) The first necessity is that of the same number of grains per bundle, of contained per container, so long as only one of the distributions (that for S or that for D) is involved. This invariance is necessary if the relation between container and contained is to be established; (b) These relations are both necessary and sufficient to ensure the permanence of the whole: $n(p$ of $g)=T$, (c) The fact that such a distribution exists implies necessarily its possible transformation into another one within the same whole: $n(p$ of $g)=n'$ of $g')=T'$, which the subject tests out by means of reciprocal pairwise projections (the surplus method). (d) These quantitative variances imply compensations that can be verified and even approximately predicted (more $p>$ fewer g per p, etc.).

But these necessities are in no way predicted and come to be recognized only to the extent that subjects understand the reasons for their actions and their consequences. These subjects nevertheless comprehend immediately that one distribution can be substituted for another while conserving the same whole. This understanding brings about the other necessities, but there is one fundamental restriction: that of reasoning about observables interpreted as containers. The contained, left unspecified in the abstract, or the addition of new variables brings about perturbations.

The critical problem for the development of multiplication is thus how to explain the change at levels IIB and IIIA from a mode of reasoning centered on the bundles or containers, observable and separate, to one in which containers become multipliers and contained multiplicands. We claim that this is in no way an unexpected mutation or abrupt modification of the way the relations are conceptualized: the purely numerical relation $4 \times 3 = 12$ maintains 4 as a containing element, but in a nonfigurative sense that contains the three unities as contained elements. These relations or correspondences remain the same whether we are dealing with material or mental objects (with all intermediate cases between the two); the three unities, similarly, remain as contained elements by virtue of the same correspondences recurring in all four 4's.

At each of our levels, we distinguish three phases in the way subjects manipulate the task: one where they are concerned with the whole; another with the parts or subsystems, which we called variously bundles or containers or, at the final level, multipliers; and the third with the elements or grains representing the contained with respect to the parts. Our hypothesis is, then, that each of these levels involves inclusion relations, but that they differ essentially in terms of their system of representation—in the degree of abstraction characterizing the nestings. Level IIA sees objects (grains) grouped into bundles: in this case, the terms *container* and *contained* take on a spatial, even a figurative sense. At the other extreme, at the level of purely numerical multiplication, such as $4 \times 3 = 12$, each of the four multipliers (this is the appropriate term to use at this level) dominates its own subsystem or part in parallel, without intersecting with the other three; they have internal structure, which gives them the status of container. But its character has nothing spatial or figurative, except insofar as the correspondences involved can be represented by arrows, as shown in the following schema:

in which the four multipliers and their correspondences, which they determine, remain in a sense containers and the multiplicands are contained.

Briefly, multiplication consists in the composition of inclusion relations—that is, correspondences of one to several. At level IIA, some of these correspondences are directly observed from the data and others are constructed (the pairwise projections of surplus elements, etc.). Such behaviors allow us to speak of multiplication in action or at least of a precursor mechanism. At levels IIB, IIIA, and IIIB, the role of constructed correspondences increases progressively; we still find trial-and-error behavior when new variables have to be coordinated, as in commutative associativity. But the figurative container is now entirely replaced by a network of numerical correspondences (this accounts for the frequent difficulty of going from the computational back to the concrete mode, as in Dan's $8 = 24 \div 3$). But from one level to the next in this evolution (once the three levels of elements, parts, and the whole are well distinguished), there is functional continuity in the search for necessities inherent in inclusion relations. This continuity seems a better candidate for explaining the distinction between multiplication and addition than are the usual criteria applied in a more or less arbitrary way.

As for associativity in multiplication, it comes into play in the two kinds of situations studied in this chapter, either in its classical or some other form. The first situation is one in which the number of nestings (levels) remains constant and only the value of the content (=contained) varies as follows: $np = n'p'$, with compensation between the values of n and p. We spoke in this case of *quantitative substitution*, which, as we have seen, constitutes itself in direct association (solidarity) with the comprehension of multiplication as such (level IIA). The second situation is one in which one level is added to the hierarchy (the number of meals) and the interplay of compensations is consequently more troublesome to regulate. Hence the developmental delay in successful performance (levels IIB and III), in spite of the fact that the meaning of inclusion relations remains the same as in simple multiplication and a fortiori in multiplicative substitution. But since there are more of them, the conservation of the whole requires not just one quantitative substitution but several of different ranks (grains and bundles, bundles and meals, meals and the total amount), which have to be carried out simultaneously. This difficulty is analogous to the one that characterizes the change from a substitution of classes to the complete set of parts (a construction also found at level III). In this second form of associativity, which one may call *associative commutativity*, the subject's task is to bring about the equality of totals, whereas in simple associativity she only has to decide whether totals are conserved.

It is now evident what the reasons are for these difficulties. The first is that in the first task, there is only one compensation to be performed, that of a lower number of grains per bundle, which necessarily has to be compensated for by a greater number of bundles. In the present case, however, the compensation to be performed is between the number of meals, that of grains per bundle, and that of the bundles themselves in order to keep constant the total of 24; dividing this number by 3 (meals) one obtains 8, which represents the product of the number of bundles (per meal) and their associated grains, i.e., 4×2. This is the source of one of the difficulties. The second follows directly from the first: the bundles have a dual role to play in these compositions, being both containers (for the grains) and contained (for the meals)—that is, they are both multipliers and multiplicands. This is the essential characteristic of these second-order multiplications required by multiplicative, commutative associativity. It is, therefore, not surprising that this second task is successfully performed at a later age than are the preceding tasks, considering the greater number and complexity of the compositions required, with their relativization of the relations between contained and containing in the case of the bundles.

Supplement: The Multiplicative Nature of Repeated Injective Correspondences

Along with the preceding experiments, we used an additional one as a control. To verify the multiplicative nature of procedures followed in correspondences, we decided to study again in terms of containers and contained (bundles and grains) the problems we studied in 1963 with B. Inhelder concerning multiplicative inequalities resulting from repeated correspondences.* For example, a subject of level IIA (Graf, 6;11) was already able to say with reference to a two-to-one correspondence that if one recipient (visible) contains 4 elements, there must then be 8 in the other one (hidden); if 6, then 12, if 10, then 10; "and when the [hidden] glass is full, the other one would go up to where?" *Half.*

In the present study, the experimenter and the child simultaneously assembled a bundle of three and one of two grains, respectively. This is repeated a number of times, and with at least one of the sides being hidden, the child is asked whether both have the same number of grains and whether, if one continues like that for a long time, there would be equality. The aim of the analyses is then to find out whether the inequalities resulting from this injective correspondence, two to three, are conceptualized as additions focused on the increase in the number of grains or as multiplications focused on the relation *container* times *contained.*

At level I, we find a mixture of unsuccessful and partially successful results. Mur (6;7), classed previously at level IB, argues that 3×3 (visible) will give the same number of grains as 3×2 (hidden) *because we both took them at the same time.* We simplify to 3×1 (experimenter) and 3×2 (subject): the same response. "How many do you have?" She counts: *six.* "And I [hidden] also have six?" *Yes.* "Look." [Surprise] *Three!* We go on to 3×3 and 3×2: she takes into account the inequality and attributes more to 3×3. "How many do you have [hidden]?" *Six* [correct]. "And on my side?" *Seven.* We go on to 4×2 against 4×3: The answer is 8 and 9. It can be seen that the reasoning remains altogether additive. In contrast, Sop II (5;7), classified before as intermediate between IB and IIA, for 4×3 and 4×2 says immediately: *You have more because you take 3 by 3 and I take 2 by 2.* "If we go on like that all afternoon, we would have the same?" *No, you take 3 by 3. . . .* "What does it make now?" *You take 3 and then 2, that makes 5, and me 2 + 1, that makes 3.* "Why 3 and 5?" *Because you take 3 by 3.* "And we will never have the same?" *No.* "Sure?" *I'm sure.* "Even without

---

*J. Piaget et al., "La formation des raisonnements récurrenciels," *Etudes d'épistémologie génétique,* vol. 17 (Paris: Presses Universitaire de France, 1963), chap. II, 5.

having tried?" *Even without having tried*[!]. It can be seen that, in spite of her unchanging capacity to see the necessity of equality, the calculation remains additive. Rob (6;5) does not know: *You have to count to know*.

At level IIA, which interests us particularly with respect to the relations established between containing and contained, Dom (7;1) says: *I'll always have less because I always make smaller bundles*. "And like that [3×3 vs. 3×2]?" *I have less* [he counts]: *six*. "And I [hidden]?" *Nine*. "How did you find 9?" *Because you put up 3 for each bundle you put up 1*. "And if each of us takes another bundle [4×3 vs. 4×2]? How many do you have?" *Eight*. "And I [hidden]?" *Twelve, because you always put 1 away*. "How many bundles did you put under there?" *Perhaps 5*. Cori (7;7) similarly infers from 6=(3×2) visible to 9 hidden grains; *and if one does it again it goes from 9 to 12*. Chri (8;4), for 2×3 and 2×2: "How many bundles do you have to take to have the same as me?" *One*. Bea (8;11), given (7×3 vs. 7×2), says that *D* would get less *even if we do it a million times*, because it's the same number of bundles but not the same number of grains. (6×3 and 6×2): "Count mine." *Eighteen*. "Yours [hidden]?" *Twelve*. "How did you do it?" *I took 2 by 2*. "How did you know when to stop?" *Because we've picked up 6 times, I've done 6×2=12*. "How many times would you have to pick up grains to have the same amount?" *Three times* [i.e., 3 bundles], *because 12+2+2+2 is 18*. Oli (9;10), for 10×3 vs. 10×2: "If we went on till tomorrow?" *I'm dead certain* [that I would always have less]. *Right from the start you took out 3 and I only 2. There will always be more* [difference]. *When you have 18, I'll have 12, and that has to go on like that*. "And if you have 12 and I have 18, if you also want to have 18?" He picks 9 bundles of 2 and counts. *You put out 6 times and I put out 9*.

From level IIB on, the procedure is immediately numerical. Dan (9;7), for 6×3 and 6×2, says that he needs 3 more bundles to equalize *because 6×3=18 and 6×2=12*; so 3 more bundles *because 9×2 makes 18*. Similar results obtained for level III. Yva (10;10), to equalize 10×2 to 10×3, says: *That takes 5 . . . 5 bundles*. "How?" *You take 10, I* [calculate] *3×10=30 and 2×10=20; I have to take half* [of 10]=5.

In the multiplication task, where the whole was to be conserved (4×3=6×2), what had to be modified was the number of bundles per partner to assure an equal number of grains for each. This problem was solvable by the method of projective correspondence used at level IIA, which we have interpreted as a kind of multiplication in action. In contrast, in the present task the number of containers (bundles) remains the same for each partner, increasing from one move to the next as long as the game continues. Each time, there is inequality of contained elements. The question is whether subjects will conserve this inequality or whether it will be seen to increase in the process and in what manner. We saw that Mur (and many others) at level I believed that this inequality comes from the injective correspondence 2<3, hence increases by 1 at each turn. These subjects cannot see that the increase is cumulative and a function of the number n of bundles ($\delta = n$ if they differ by 1 element, $\delta = 2n$ if they differ by 2; this question was not explicitly asked, since the relation $\delta = n$ was already difficult enough when the bundles differed by one element!). In short, the inequality increases with the number of containers. Subjects at level IIA understand this when they infer that if one partner has 6 grains, the other must have 9 (hidden); if one has 8, the other has 12; when one has 12, the other has 18; etc.

In this case, the number of containers or bundles takes on an entirely different functional meaning of explaining the increase in contained elements (grains), and it clearly functions as a multiplier in action (facilitated by the relation of containing to contained rather than between any arbitrary multiplicands). Cor (7;7) already uses the word *times*; "a million times," says Bea, and "6 times and me 9," declares Oli. Dan (11;3), at level III, sums it up by saying: "I took 6 times 2 and you 6 times 3 grains, so you have 6 more," expressing the implicit principle subjects had already used at level IIA, which is why we have spoken of multiplication in action.

In general, multiplication is addition of additions, but the latter can be conceived of in two quite different ways: either subjects add the results of the various additions, which is simply additive behavior; or, they come to realize (sometimes even by counting) that the number n of additions corresponds to the number of operations and that, therefore, this number represents a multiplier. This understanding does not depend on numerical calculations ($n \times n'$), which come into play at level IIB and which at that level, and even more so at level III, come to be thematic and the only procedure used.

7

Distributivity

with A. Henriques-Christophides

This chapter will deal with distributivity in multiplication as found in adding two values — that is, with the fact that an increase (xh) of the whole $(A+B)$ proceeds homogeneously over the parts, such that $n(A+B)=nA+nB$. In this case, we are dealing with a conditional necessity that is common to many numerical, spatial, and even physical structures. Previous research (with G. Cellerier) on the extension of an elastic had shown that, in the phyiscal domain, this pro-structure is a late acquisition (there is a long phase when subjects localize the extension at the endpoint without seeing the homogeneity in the lengthening of all parts of the object).* We decided to investigate whether this distributivity is understood more easily in the arithmetical and the spatial domain. As an operation, it is complex because it consists in establishing the equivalence between the multiplication of the whole and the addition of the multiplied parts, i.e., in a composition between multiplications and additions — not even considering the problem of dissociating the whole $A+B$ from its parts A and B. This dissociation in itself implies the conservation of the whole, whereas distributivity as such requires the conservation of the increases, which is quite a different matter.

One of the questions to be treated concerns differences in difficulty between two kinds of methods that seem to be based on the same principles. Another problem concerns the differences and similarities between the results obtained with discrete vs. continuous data.

Section I: The Distributivity of Discrete Items

Two different tasks were used. The first, which we call *CT* (candy task), consists of presenting bundles of candy, three together, two at a time, or one by one. The subject first receives a bundle of three candies and has to verify its equiva-

---

*See J. Piaget and R. Garcia, *Understanding Causality* (New York: Norton, 1974).

lence with a bundle of two plus one single candy. Then we give subjects n bundles of three ($n=2$, 3, or 4, etc.) while the experimenter takes n bundles of two plus one single candy. The equation $3=2+1$ thus specifies the initial relation of the whole to the parts, and the subsequent increases xn represent distributivity to the extent that subjects comprehend their identical multiplicative effects.

The second task, which we call BT (bean task), uses two big boxes. The first one contains a few beans (a small number) inserted by the experimenter, whereas the second one is empty; the child has to insert double (or triple) the amount by putting in two (or three, etc.) beans each time the adult adds one to her box (which she does successively after the initial presentation). We designate the experimenter's box as $(A+B)$ and the subject's as $n(A+B)$. The experimenter then distributes her beans $(A+B)$ into two small, empty boxes, one containing A, the other B beans. After this (or at the same time), the child also receives two small, empty boxes that are placed under her first box $n(A+B)$. She is asked to put nA beans into one of the boxes, taken from a reserve (i.e., $n=2$, 3, etc.), where n remains constant over a series of trials and identical to n in $n(A+B)$. In this way, the subject doubles (or triples, etc.) the parts A and B in the same way as she had done for the whole by increasing $(A+B)$ to $n(A+B)$. The question is whether the subject perceives the equivalence between $(nA+nB)$ and $n(A+B)$, no longer having to be concerned with the boxes initially filled by the experimenter. The relation $n(A+B)=nA+nB$ here represents the distributivity of sets of increasing discrete elements. We shall present two analogous tasks for continuous items after having described the developmental levels for tasks CT and BT.

Level I

At this initial level, subjects fail both CT and BT. They make no reference to any transformation and only judge by looking at results, which they evaluate perceptually or in terms of number of bundles. In other cases, they refuse to make a decision without counting the beans.

Cri (6;7) receives a bundle of 3, while the experimenter takes $2+1$: *That makes the same amount because $2+1$ makes 3, and there, there are 3 candies.* "Bravo! How many bundles of 3 would you like?" *Four* [she takes them]. "And I take 4 bundles of 2 and 4 single ones. We have the same?" *We have to count to find out.* "Good [the pair 4 of 3 vs. 4 of 2 and 4 of 1 is repeated]. *There* [$2+1$], *there is more.* "Why?" She points to the bundles. "O.K., we will play again. Take what you like." She takes 2 bundles of 2, 2 of 3, and 2 single candies. "And I'll take that [4 of 3]." *You took less; you took 4 and I took 2 each time, so that makes more.* We return to 2 bundles of 3 for her and 2 times put underneath a bundle of 2 and a single candy: *It's you that has more: each time you took 2 and I only that* [she starts counting]. *Oh! That still makes the same!* We play again with 5 of 3 and 5 of 2 plus 5 unities: *We have to count, because it gets mixed up*. *BT*. *If you count the two boxes together, there will be more there* [two boxes] *and less there* [one box. "Are you sure?" *Yes, because there, there are two boxes, and here there is only one*.

Lua (6;9), BT: She thinks that *there will be more* in $2(A+B)$ and that *there is less* in $2A+2B$ together *because we've put more things there than there*. "How do you know?" *I counted them* [one of the two boxes], *there are 6*. "And there?" *I did not count* [but I saw that] *it makes 12 there*. "And the two together?" *There is less*. "Sure?" *Yes*. We start over, obtaining the same result.

Kat (7;1), CB: *I have 3 and you 2 and 1: that makes 3 too*. She then takes 3 bundles of 3 and the experimenter takes 3 bundles of 2 and 3 unities: *There isn't the same*, but then she reconsiders by repeating that $3=2+1$. We start again with (5×3) against $(5\times2)+(5\times1)$: *We have the same amount because you have taken 5 candies* [=bundles] *with 3, and then another time 5 of 3. Then after, you took 5 ones and 5 with 2, so that made 5 everywhere*. Her way of seeing equality is thus based on the number of times (5) the same actions are performed and not on the relationship between container and contained. *BT*: *This is where there is more* [in the single box] *if they're not together, and, if they are together, it's there* [two boxes] *where there are more*.

These kinds of reactions are general in the youngest subjects. They clearly indicate the obstacles to be overcome, hence the conditions that must be met to attain distributivity. First, it is evident that the additions must be conserving (conservation of the addends as well as their sum). Now, Kat denies conservation explicitly: "Therre is more . . . if they're [the addends] not together," but there are fewer if they are put together; for this subject, the value of the sum depends, thus, only on the number of bundles. For Lua, the item $2(A+B)$ makes more than $2A+2B$ "because we've put more things" into the one box. In fact, as soon as there are too many, "it gets mixed up" (Cri). The general fact, which is common to both types of contradictory opinions, is thus the difficulty of mastering the relation between container and contained: Kat even designates with the same expression, "five candies," the bundles themselves. Most importantly, although these subjects are well able to say that $3=2+1$, they lose this equation as soon as there is iteration to $n(3)=n(2)+n(1)$. Kat neglects the contained elements to the point of inferring a general equality from the fact that 5 (parts) were used on each side—i.e., the same multiplier (same action) was repeated. She even reports one too many, most probably because she confuses what the experimenter keeps with what she gives to the suybject, paying no attention to the multiplicands. In short, since neither multiplication nor addition is mastered yet, it is not surprising that distribution, which composes them into a single system, is not understood, in spite of subjects' initial affirmation that $3=2+1$, since this remains a local insight that is not generalized to conserving additions. What's more, it is not applied to multiplicative increases, as would be required for distributivity as an equally conserving pro-structure.

Level II

The reactions of this second level (from 7 and 8 to 9 and 10 years, and often even 10 years of age) remain intermediate and probing. We find, not surprisingly, that responses to *CT* are more advanced than those to *BT*. The problem with *BT* is that subjects frequently entertain an even systematic belief to the effect that a whole, by virtue of its greater size, grows more than does the sum of the parts, which seem weaker: what we have to analyze, then, is a kind of false proportionality and its relation to true proportionality:

Dev (7;10), *CT*: three bundles of 3 vs. $(3 \times 2) + (3 \times 1)$. "Who has more?" *No one.* (5×3) vs. $(5 \times 2) + (5 \times 1)$: *One has to count.* (3×3) vs. $(3 \times 2) + (3 \times 1)$: *We have the same. BT: They are the same, because we have always taken 2 and 2.* But he is unable to reproduce the game: *You take 1 and I take 2* [he does this several times]. "Is it finished?" *Yes.* We start over: *There is less there* [the single box, $n(A+B)$. "How do you do it?" *I don't know. By chance.*

Tal (8;10), *CT*: Even though she naturally declared that $3 = 2 + 1$, she chooses too fast 6, then 10 bundles of 3 and gets mixed up trying to equalize 6 and 10, using 2 bundles of two and one. But with 4 bundles of three candies, she puts $2 + 1$ under each bundle. We proceed to 7 of 3 vs. 7 of 2 and 7 singles, and she immediately concludes: *You have the same as me. . . . You put them together and you have the same as me.* However, in *BT*, with its simple duplications: *There are more there* [nA and nN]. "Why?" *Because there are two boxes. There* [single box], *there's less.*

The candy task, *CT*, is already mastered at 7–8 years (see also Nic below). Equalization is obtained either by establishing term-by-term correspondences between the three-element bundles and the pairs, $2 + 1$, or by decomposing the three elements into $2 + 1$. Since these equalities are reiterated with comprehension of the relations between containing and contained, these reactions can be seen as *multiplications in action* (in the sense defined in chapter 6). We may, therefore, already speak of distributing. But the bean task, *BT*, which includes a greater number of containers, leads to a variety of errors and partial successes at this level unless it is preceded by the candy task, *CT*.

Mar (7;6) may well declare in the beginning that $3 = 2 + 1$, but later she says either that *there is more here* [$nA + nB$] *because we have poured that one into that one* [= mixture nA and nB) or *there is more here because there are two more boxes* [nA and nB, separately].

Ile (8;5): *There is less in these two boxes than in that one* [$nA + nB$]. "Sure?" *Yes. There are 8 and here. . . . No, it's the same.* Then: *If you take these two boxes at the same time, there is more.*

Lip (8;9) describes the actions correctly. "So between these two taken together, and that one?" *It makes less* [parts]. "And in that one [whole]?" *So that makes . . . 6 and 6 . . . so, that is equal.* "Are you sure, or is it better to count?" *It's better to count.*

Pin (9;8): *No, it's not the same. That is a lot because there are two boxes.* We put them together. *Here it's more* [A and B together, vs. A+B].

Bea (9;9): *Here it's more: it's not because there are two boxes, but we've put more in.* "Do you want to count?" *Fourteen everywhere!* "How is that?" We start over with 3: *The same.* "How do you know?" *I don't know.*

Ton (10;10): *I think that there is more here* [whole]. "Why?" *Because you've put in less. . . . Wait: there are more there* [two boxes]. He counts and finds them equal. We start again with 3: *I think here* [the whole], *it's more.*

Xan (10;0) defends the following thesis: *There where you've put them all together, that's where there are more beans.*

But in addition to these cases, where, up to 10 years of age, subjects still affirm inequality in favor of the number of bundles or, more interestingly, the whole where we've "put all together" (Ile and Xan), we also find, even at 7 to 9 years, some subjects who succeed in equalization by invoking either the actions in their correct order or conservation of the initial totals. These more advanced subjects have begun, in contrast to the preceding ones, with the candy task, which has provided them with a kind of learning as to the relations between containing and contained:

Ton (7;10) begins by hesitating, and concludes: *It's the same.* "What makes you say that?" *If I took the two boxes and emptied them into that one* [one box], *it would be the same.* "Sure?" *Yes.*

Nic (8;10) affirms equality for 3 bundles in *CT.* "Now you take 30 bundles of 3 and I take 30 bundles of 2 and 30 of 1, who has more?" *No, we have the same, because you have 2 and 1, I have 3, but I divide them up: if I put 2 there and 1 there, it makes the same. That would be the same, even if one had 30.* "And 300?" He laughs. *It's always the same. BT: I think I have the same* [$n(A+B)=nA+nB$] *because you gave me in one turn what I have here in two turns. Unless I am mistaken.* "Some kids say that the first time it makes more." *I say it comes to the same.*

Iva (9;1): *It's the same*, justifying this in terms of an ordered enumeration of actions.

In brief, one finds at this level of concrete operations generalized success on the candy task, *CT*, accompanied by failure at task *BT* because of absence of generalization (Mar and Tal) or of success at that task mediated by comprehension of embeddings and conservations. In contrast, subjects who did not do the *CT* first (all subjects from Mar to Xan) generally fail the *BT*. This can be explained with reference to the fact that the additive compositions in that task involve a greater number of multipliers or containers than in the *CT*.

Level III

At about 10–12 years of age, subjects can succeed at *BT* without being prepared by *CT*. They base their judgments on an analysis of actions, conservations, or numerical multiplication; they occasionally invoke associativity of addition in their arguments:

Van (10;10): *The same thing: Each time you put in a bean, I put in 2, that should make double the number. The way you divided it here, it's simply put into two boxes. It's clear that it is the same.* By three: *If you put in 5, I put in 15. Then you divide it up into 7 and 8.* "I divide it?" *Yes, 2 and 3. For me, 6 and 9. Yes, that makes 15.*

Car (11;3): *The same, because each time you've put in 1, I've put in 2. Then we started over again, but with only one box. So it makes the same number.* "You can explain that with numbers?" He then writes in a line *1,1,1, . . . ,10* and underneath *2,2,2, . . . ,20*. After that he writes *1,1,1,1,1* apart, and again *1,1,1,1,1* apart (i.e., 5+5) and underneath *2,2,2,2,2* and again the same number, thus 10+10, showing that the products 20 and 20 are the same.

Ori (11;9): *We have exactly the same amount* [in $n(A+B)$ as in $[nA+nB]$. *You put one there* $[A+B]$ *and I two* [in $n(A+B)$]. *Then you told me to divide this and put it into the little boxes, and I put in 2 each time, so it comes to exactly the same thing.* "Certain?" *Absolutely.* "Can you explain it to me?" *Yes, but not with the beans.* She then draws (in small circles): *You: 1 1 1→(11)+1. Me: 1 1 1 1 1 1→1 1 1 1+(11)*, which is precisely the additive composition of multipliers, $n+2$.

Bra (11;9) justifies her judgment of equality by means of a description of the actions but also, like Ori, shows her comprehension with a drawing of small circles, which we designate by their numbers 4→8, compared with 1→2 and 3→6, hence the equality 8=2+6.

Dan (12;0): *It's the same thing, because 24 and 24=48—that is,* $nA+nB=n(A+B)$.

None of the subjects states in the abstract that multiplying a whole by a number $n-n(A+B)-$is equivalent to multiplying its parts A and B by the same number n, which would amount to constructing a thematic of distributivity in general: but each of them understands this relation. Car, Ori, and Bra even formulate it, eloquently and without hesitation, by a drawing. This attests to the presence of a new necessity, which was attained at level IIB only on *CT* and remained in a state of preparation on *BT*. We shall return to this point at the end of section II.

Section II: The Distributivity of Continuous Elements

To the two methods *CT* and *BT*—the results of which, just described, were rather different—we added two other procedures of a similar structure but involving continuous items, surfaces, and lengths; these could have certain, perhaps facilitating effects on subjects' performance. Instead of candies, we used squares (task *ST*) to be cut down into pieces, *P*. The question is whether the sum of the squares, nS, is equivalent to that of their parts, nP taken together. The analog to this in task *CT* is the equivalence between $n(A+B)$ and $nA+nB$. As for the more complex nestings of *BT*, we have replaced them by a task requiring the composition of lengths, *LT*, using strips of paper. In this task, a total length, *C*, distributed into parts, $A+B=C$, gets lengthened to nC while its parts are lengthened separately into $A \rightarrow nA$ and $B \rightarrow nB$. The question is again whether nC (the total set *A* and *B*) is equivalent to $nA+nB$, the individual increases in length, using identical multipliers *n*.

Two interesting results were obtained. The difficulties are the same with the continuous as with the discrete items, in particular between *LT* and *BT*; and there is the same difference between *LT* and *ST* as was noted between *BT* and *CT*. The tasks *LT* and *BT* were noticeably more difficult. These similarities are both reassuring for the experimenter and instructive for the analysis of distributivity.

The Squares Task

The child is given two big sheets of paper and asked to cut out two equal squares (about 5 cm^2), one for herself and the other for the experimenter. The experimenter cuts her square into 3 rectangles while the child adds to hers 3 or 4 other squares of the same size (5 cm^2). Then she cuts out another series of 9 rectangles in sets of 3 equivalent to each of the 3 new squares. These she hands to her partner. Thus the child would have, for example, 4 big squares and the adult 12 rectangles (her 3 initial ones plus the 9 received from the subject). The question is then to decide whether the total figure of 4 squares belonging to the child is of the same size as the 12 pieces, put together, of the experimenter.

Here are four examples of level 1:

Cri (6;7) agrees that 3 pieces make a square, thus the same amount for a mouse to eat. But with 6 pieces against 2 squares, it would have more: "More pieces or more to eat?" *More to eat.* Then she changes her mind about her initial response: [A square and 3 pieces], *if you put them together neatly maybe it's the same, but now they're cut, there are 3 there and one there, that makes more to eat.*

Tin (6;11), with 2 squares and 6 pieces ($n=2$ for the whole and the parts): *It's not the same anymore, you have more to eat.*

At 7 years, some subjects still hesitate. The most striking response is that by Col (8;10): With 4 squares and 12 pieces, *It's you that has more: 12 is more than 4.* "Look again." *Ah! but there is also the size! So, it's you that has the smallest carpet, but if it's by calculation* [=number], *then you have the biggest.*

But, from 7 years on, the answers tend to be correct, either spontaneously or in the end.

Tia (7;1): *We have the same because, if you put them together* [the first 3 pieces] *it makes that square there, and if you put all of them together, it makes that one there. Look, I'll stick them back together.* "And if you don't stick them together?" *We would still have the same.* We can see here the transition from $C=P+P'+P''$ to $nC=nM+nM'+nM''$, etc. —that is, distributivity in action.

Vid (7;10): *It's the same because if I cut them in 2, it would be the same.* "But now I have 6?" *That doesn't matter.*

Har (8;10): *You have more papers because you have cut yours. But we both have the same.*

Van (9;11): *Three put together, that makes a square. All the small ones together, that makes four squares.*

We see the close analogy between this task and *CT* with respect to the initial errors and the subsequent successes observed.

The Lengths Task

We cut out a thin strip of paper, about 10 cm long, and ask the subject to make one that is twice as long.* After that, the experimenter cuts hers into two unequal segments, A and B. Her initial strip thus has the value $(A+B)$ as a single whole and the child's the value $2(A+B)$. Following this, we ask the child to double each part separately, A to $2A$ and B to $2B$. The problem is then to determine whether there is equality between $2(A+B)$ and $2A+2B$, or, more generally, between $n(A+B)$ and $nA+nB$. The subject could glue nA and nB back together to find out. It can be seen that this task is isomorphic with *BT*. Here follow some examples of level I:

Nat (6;2) does not agree that $(A+B)=A+B$ separated, since A by itself is *a pretty big piece*, nor, especially, that $nA+nB$ glued back together give the same value as $n(A+B)$. *I'd say that* [these], *it's a bit bigger. . . . No, a bit smaller.*

Lua (6;2): *A and B, it's bigger, because there are 2 pieces.*

At 7–10 years of age (normally level II), one finds the same difficulties:

Col (7;4) says that $2A$ and $2B$ are *bigger because it was made longer.*

Dal (7;5), after success with *ST*, generalizes to *LT*: *It's the same, because it was double here* [2 $(A+B)$] *and these two* [$2A$ and $2B$] *are double of these two* [A and B].

Mar (7;10) hypothesizes equality but by qualitative compensations: *The same, because we've cut two bigger pieces and 1 to 4 smaller ones.* "Are you sure it's the same?" *Hm.* "What's to be done?" *Measure them.*

Phi (8;5): *The whole* [$2(A+B)$] *is a bit bigger than that* [$2A+2B$].

---

*And which we leave half rolled up to avoid purely perceptual judgments.

Pin (9;8): *Perhaps that* [2A and 2B], *they're bigger, and that* [the whole] *smaller.*

Bea (9;9) says of 2A+2B: *It's smaller.*

Until 10 years of age, subjects encounter the same difficulties as those at level I, but the squares task presents no more problems. The relationship between CT and ST is thus the same as that between BT and CT. We shall now present a few cases at level III, beginning with Van, whose performance at BT was clearly level III but who still shows some hesitation with LT:

Van (10;10): *It's the same length, because we haven't used two strips* [new ones for A and B]: *We've used only one strip, the same.* "Sure?" *Yes, I think I'm certain, but not sure.* "What about [2(A+B)=2A+2B, repeating the actions]?" *Yes, yes, it's the same.* "Sure?" *Not very.*

Car (11;3): *The same length because it's made with the same piece of paper, cut in 2, and each time there was double the length.* "Would you like to compare?" *No, if one has calculated right* [=reasoned], *then it's the same length.*

Ema (11;4): *The same length, because we've taken the whole strip, then I took the double, then we've broken it in two, and I've doubled the small* [part] *and the bigger one: so that comes to the same.*

We see the clarity of reasoning, and it is surprising that it takes this advanced level of operational development to perform these relatively simple deductions, and surprising to find a subject like Van still having doubts about their logical necessity.

Section III: Conclusions

The type of necessity that characterizes the solutions of the tasks BT and LT is apparently of a superior rank and thus "stronger" than that attested by successful performance at CT and ST. To prove this, one must first see precisely how these tasks differ. In CT and ST, the initial whole is conserved in the course of the operations that follow: the three-item bundles in CT and the large square belonging to the child in ST only get to be repeated, since the initial model remains constantly available. In contrast, in BT and LT, the initial whole gets changed from the start: the whole A+B of the experimenter becomes disconnected in A and B, whereas the child doubles or multiplies it by n to yield $n(A+B)$. Similarly, the strip of paper in LT is divided by the adult, and the subject doubles or multiplies these parts. The result is that in CT and ST, distributivity finds its support in the conservation of the whole, which markedly facilitates the comprehension of relations; whereas in BT and LT, it is the increase xn that needs to be conserved. This is a very different problem. In fact, it is not at all implausible to assume, as do Ile, Ton, and Xan at level II, that a single, large multiplicand (here the whole) might proportionally show greater increases than do several small ones, when multiplied by the same number (2), or inversely, several multiplicands, even though small, might lead to a greater product than a single one that was initially larger.

We are dealing here with false proportionalities; nevertheless, implicit in these reactions is an appeal to proportions. The correct proportionality involved in our case of distributivity is:

$$\frac{n(A+B)}{A+B} = \frac{nA}{A} = \frac{nB}{B} = \frac{nA+nB}{A+B}$$

These relations are clearly involved in comprehending the distributivity in BT and LT (hence the difficulties encountered up to level III, the level at which proportionality is constructed), but they do not play the same role in CT and ST because of the support afforded by the conservation of the initial whole.

In short, distributivity consists in understanding the homogeneity of the increases of the whole and the parts. In the case of CT, where candies are grouped in bundles of 3, 2, or 1, and that of ST, where squares are divided into thirds, the increases xh are the result of iterations amounting to copying n times a model that remains visible and where the equality of the whole and the parts can easily be verified. In contrast, in BT and LT the whole is doubled separately and then divided into parts, which get multiplied in turn. In this case, it is no longer possible to establish a correspondence between a model and its copies, nor even, unless by inference, to make sure that the new whole is really equivalent to the union of the double (or triple, etc.) parts. Consequently, in this situation the homogeneity of increases can only be of an inferential nature and must be based on explicit reasons (as at level III), whereas in CT and ST it derives from perceptible iterations. The successes observed at level II on these tasks do not go beyond the status of distributivity in action.

Putting aside these differences, we see that the necessity involved in distributivity goes largely together with an integrative process: each and every one of the additive and multiplicative operations required in the solution of the preceding tasks is, in itself, very simple. However, their composition is far from simple, since what has to be added are increases. This explains the complexity of their integration within a total system, a higher order system compared with that of associativity.

8

Necessary and Sufficient Conditions in the Construction of Proofs

with C. Brulhart and S. Dionnet (Section I) and A. Henriques-Christophides (Section II

After having analyzed the forms of necessity inherent in causal and spatial relations (chapters 1–4) and in the general modes of composition or pro-structures (chapters 5–7), we shall now study those inferential mechanisms that best represent logical necessity. But since all logico-mathematical reasoning is inherently necessary, and since we have already spent many years studying their operational structures, what remains to be done to understand necessity is to focus on the simplest forms of verification that are also the most instructive ones from a developmental viewpoint – that is, the elaboration of proofs. The problem chosen in this chapter is one of the simplest that can be imagined. It concerns only correspondences.

Section I: The Necessary and Sufficient in a Problem of Successive Integrations

The experimenter has at her disposal a large, very irregular and closed figure consisting of 13 sides, of which 12 are linked by lines forming various angles; one curved line connects the remaining 2 sides of the figure. This figure remains hidden under 20 rectangular covers, which the child may lift one after another as she pleases (figure 1). She also has before her 12 similar figures, only one of which is identical to the hidden model. The problem is simply to find it by eliminating all the others (figure 2).

All forms of necessity result from compositions, of which there are three aspects: determination (necessary and sufficient conditions), elaboration (reasons), and amplification (consequences). The solution of the problem presented here mainly concerns – with respect to the proofs to find – the first of these aspects of necessity. It seems important to study it at all age levels. In addition, the problem allows one to analyze the *strength* of the necessities invoked, beginning with a low degree (necessary, but more or less insufficient conditions) and

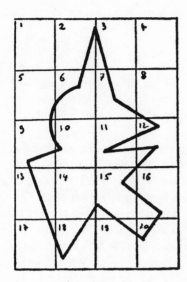

Fig. 1

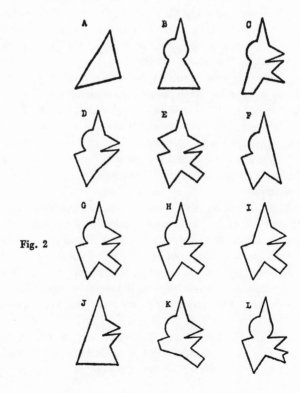

Fig. 2

proceeding to upper levels (necessary conditions that are justified as being sufficient).

Levels IA and IB

The two essential characteristics of level IA are the absence of any kind of proof and a lack of coordination of the different indices, which remain unintegrated within a whole so that subjects forget the earlier ones when they pass on to other clues:

Fab (5;10) picks up cover 2 (revealing a slanted line, which is common to all 12 figures): *It's the* A, *the* J. "What about some others?" *It could be the* I. "What do you want to do?" *Pick up the 6* [underneath cover 2] *to see the other part of the design* [builds out of it a small section of the upper left of the figure]. *That is the* I. "Why?" *Because there is the bar. Oh, no, it's the* D. "Only that one?" *The* D *because it has the same thing as the* G [points to the curved line] *and those two* [L *and* H]. "Do you know which?" *No.* "What can you do to be sure?" *Put them next to the design* [the hidden model] *to see.* "What about opening another box?" He picks up 5. *It's the same. Or maybe* B, H, L, D, K, F. "Which to pick up now?" *The 9* [in line with 5], *it's the* G, H, L, F, *that's all.* "But which one is it?" *The* G, H, L, K, D. "To pick up some more, do you have to stay on this side [after 2, 6, 5, and 9]?" *The 3. It could be* G, H, L, D. *The* G *because the line is turned the same way,* etc. He even goes so far as to point to the *I*, which has no curved line.

Nat (6;6) likewise begins by picking up 2 and saying, *It's* A, *because it has the same point* [as on the hypothetical, albeit hidden, model]. "The 2 can tell you already that it is *A*?" *Then it's* G, *because there is the point.* She then opens 7: *It's* C *because there is a point and there is that* [the angle visible in 7]. Nat affirms being *completely sure* that it is *C*, but adds immediately that it could be *also* D. She then opens 6 and 11: *Yes, it's* C; then, *it's* H, *it's* D [shows the curved line]; *it's one of the two*; then *G*, but *we have to take them all off, like that one will be able to see if it's correct or not.*

Nad (6;4), among other things, gives an example of a contradiction. At one point she chooses *H*, forgetting that previously she had excluded that figure with square 7. She finds *G* only after having picked up all covers.

Unlike the preceding subjects, whose explorations were limited to the upper part of the grid and never ventured underneath the midline extending from 9 to 12, the following subjects (of level IB) endeavor to inform themselves also about the lower part of the model by picking up the covers from 13–16 and 17–20 as well:

Cla (6;10) also begins with 2 and concludes that *It's* A, then opens 3 and decides *J*, which he finds confirmed by 7. He then intends to lift *two or three more: I would like to see if it makes that* [the two points of *J*. He opens 11 and 12 and thinks his guess confirmed. Then, *I'll pick up 6 to see if there is the round* [curved line]. *Yes, it's there: it's* D. *I'll try some more because perhaps it's* B. *Oh, no, there isn't the beak.* After that: *I'd better open there still* [13 to 16!]. He lifts 16: *I was wrong, because there is a really straight line* [the lower right of the hidden model]: *It's* I! "Sure?" *Yes, but there too* [G], *it's true* [lifts 14–15]. *It's the same* [for G and I]. He lifts 13. *It's* G *because there* [9] *it's round and there* [I] *it isn't round.* "You had opened 7. Wasn't that enough for that?" *I don't remember any more.* "Could you have found it by opening fewer squares?" *No.*

Ver (6;9) lifts up altogether 2, 3, 4, 6, 5, 11, 14, 10, 13, 15, and 20. At 2, she says: *It's a piece of* C. "Only?" *The* I, *too, and the* E *and the* F, *but no others.* Only later does it strike her that *all have a point.* At 5, she thinks that it is *B,* or *G, B, H, K, L,* but not *I because it doesn't have the round bit.* At 11: *It's the* D *because there is the point* [near the bottom]. *The* G *too.* But at 13 (which is common to about six or seven figures, *D* and *G* among others) she concludes: *That should be the* G *because there is more space,* and at 15 (decisive): *Yes, that's it because there is a piece* [lower right]. Then: *We have to open number 20 to see if it continues.* When asked, she agrees that some squares are not useful—i.e., 1, 4, 9, 13, 17, 18, 19 (this is not true for 9 and 18). All the others she considers necessary *to be sure.*

Ste (7;4), in spite of his age, still proceeds by trial and error, but he remembers some of the information. At first he indicates several possible items: for 3, it is *J* or *H*; for 7, it is *I, C,* or *K*; for 6, it is *K,* or *I*, perhaps *D*; and for 5, it is *L, D, G,* or *K*, etc. But from 18 on: *I know which it is, it's* G. "Sure?" *I'm sure. No: to know for sure, I shall open 13 . . . and if I open 9, it will be more* [sure]. "Perhaps *D*?" *Yes; so I better open a box there* [lower right] *to see which is correct.* After some more hesitations (12 may give *L*): *No, it's* G, *I'm sure of it*: he confirms it with box 20. The final choice, *G*, had thus been prepared for by 5, 6, 18, 9, 12, and 20 (out of a total of 10 openings).

Level IA is thus characterized by the absence of any kind of integration and of sufficient necessity. This lack of integration manifests itself in two ways. First, the fact that exploration is limited to squares 1 to 12 shows that the subjects do not expect the hidden model to occupy the entire grid (in fact, only the squares 1, 4, and 10 are empty). When Fab lifts up 6 "to see the other part of the design," it is only to follow up box 2. Second, the exploration proceeds either randomly or step-by-step, so that the different indices never become integrated within a system. Each clue thus provides only partial information that is, therefore, common to several figures. What is particularly striking is that the possibilities are only partially exploited: none of the level IA subjects says, as Ver (IB) does, that "all have a point" at the top. Nat first indicates *A* because of this point, then when lifting 3 thinks that this confirms *A*; but she agrees that it could also be *G* "because there is a point." She does not see that this is true for all. This lack of integration of indices can even lead to contradictions, as in the case of

Nad, who chooses *H* after forgetting that she had already eliminated it with box 7. Another case is Fab, who discovers the curved line by opening 6 but later chooses *I*, the figure that does not have a curved line.

From the point of view of necessity—that is, the inferential aspect of integration—we can conclude that the level IA reactions only attain prenecessities that are nonsufficient. For the clues to be sufficient to verify the correct choice, *G*, it is necessary to coordinate the information about the left curved line with the two lower angles and those on the right, as well as with the quasi-rectangular shape of the appendage in the lower right. Each of these indices can be found in other figures. Only their combination makes the choice of *G* necessary and is sufficient for verification. This is precisely what level IA subjects do not understand, when each individual clue makes them "completely sure" (as Nat says) that it must be such-and-such a figure. This also does not prevent them from changing their mind very soon afterward. "Sure" thus means simply "sure that this may be true," and complete certainty may only be obtained under the condition as formulated by the same child, Nat: "We have to take them all off" to see "if it's correct or not."

The reactions characterizing level IB begin to show a certain degree of integration in the two ways distinguished above. The main parts of the figure are explored purposefully: Cla wants to see whether he can find the two points of *J* and then also the curve on the left. Ver explores the lower part of the grid, controlling its shape by lifting 20 after 15. The same behavior can be observed in Ste (at the end). With respect to the clues, they are now integrated locally by searches directed toward adjacencies and no longer in a step-by-step fashion. Thus, in certain points, necessity is attained at this level. First, the subjects begin to understand that sufficiency requires several clues simultaneously, that a single clue only leads to several possibilities: Ver, thus, contrasts the clues she considers useless (while making errors about 9 and 18) with those that need to be kept "to be sure." Second, "to be sure" acquires a specific meaning. Ste says that he is "sure" about *G* after having seen 18 but corrects himself immediately: "No: to know for sure, I shall open 13 . . . and . . . 9"; and he still verifies his final "I'm sure" by inspecting 20. But these acquisitions are still only partial and not thematically explicit.

Level II

With the onset of concrete operations, several kinds of progress can be observed:

Myr (7;1) has a strategy of eliminating as well as retaining possibilities revealed by the clues: 3 eliminates *I* and *E*; 6 excludes *J*; 7 excludes *L*, *B*, and *H*; 15 excludes *D*, *C*, and *K*; the excluded figures are all put into one class. Only *E*, *I*, and *G* remain (*I* has already been eliminated once, returns briefly, but gets eliminated again for its lack of a curved line). Box 5 confirms G; *that's sure. I shall still open 9* [does it]. *Now I'm sure,* but she continues opening boxes.

Tal (8;10): The experimenter removes box 2: *That could be anything, because there is a point on each.* "Which are you going to open?" *Number 16.* "What will it tell you?" *Whether it's round or straight, whether there is a beak.* "If you open number 16, can you already tell which it is?" *I don't think so* [she opens 16]. *That could be K, J, H, or G, or I or E, but not another: only those have a rectangle here* [in the lower right]. *I'll open number 7.* "Why?" *To see if it's round or whether there is a loop to the right.* She does it. *It could be D, E, I, K, J, or G.* "What about C?" *Yes, but not B, nor L, nor A, because there is no round part. I'll open 13 to see if it goes like that* < *or all straight* \ *or like that* [trapezoid]. She does it. *It's G, H, or F, E, D, L. What you can put away is B, A, J, K, and C because the line goes like that* \. She then picks up number 6 *to see if it's pointed or round* [does it]. *It's not K, it could be G or C. It's G, because it is like that and not like that* [slanted lines]. Then she compares all figures with the exposed parts of the model: *It's G.* "Sure?" *Yes, it's G.*

Pie (8;9) similarly announces what information he is going to get: Number 3 will show whether *it is bent or there may be a bit of a circle.*

Tie (8;11) specifies the following possible methods: *Open them one by one from top to bottom;* or *do the middle and then the sides.* In fact, he goes from 5 to 16 to compare the two outer edges and decides in favor of *G,* which he confirms by 14 (he had done 2, 3, and 7 before) and by item-by-item comparison between what the open squares reveal and the figure *G.* "Are you sure?" *Absolutely,* [but] *I prefer opening another one: there could still be other things, you never know.*

Pha (9;3) finds *G* after inspection of 6, 7, 15, and 17 and does not think that it could be any other. Still, in spite of her age, she declares that to be sure one would *have to open all the boxes.*

A first progress to be noted is the anticipatory character of proceeding. Thus, Tal explains in detail what she can learn by opening each of the covers. This involves a comparison between the 12 figures to choose from and the variable characteristics (of the model) to be selected: lines curving to the left or to the right, the presence and the number of "beaks," "rectangles," or their absence on both sides of the lower part, etc. Such purposeful, directed explorations presuppose a method, and this is a second kind of innovation at this level. Thus, Tal searches for useful clues, and Tie scans adjacencies: "one by one from top to bottom" or "do the middle and then the sides." A third progress is the constitution of classes, and not only of possibilities (which can already be found at level IB), but still only of excluded items: "What you can put away," says Tal, "is *B, A, J, K,* and *C*"; or, for Myr, it's *J, L, B, H,* etc. But even though subjects at this level succeed in justifying necessities by giving reasons, this level of acquisition does not attain the highest rank required in this task, which is the necessary and sufficient character of the proofs given. What distinguishes these reactions from those found at the next level is that each subject, after having declared certainty that G is correct, continues to lift new covers or to believe that an even greater certainty could be obtained by opening all the covers. Thus, Myr, after having said, "Now, I am sure," continues to open boxes. Tal, in spite of her systematic way of proceeding, in the end compares the exposed parts of the hidden model with the 12 figures presented as choices. Tie may well declare his certainty about the choice of G, but he still adds: "I prefer opening another one: there could still be other things, you never know." Now, unless there is a trick in the hidden model, it is obvious from the nature of the task that it must correspond to one of the 12 figures presented; it is thus sufficient to examine these to find all the characteristics useful to know in deciding on a choice. Even at 9 years, Pha, who finds G using the methods characteristic of this level, concludes that to be really sure one needs "to open all the boxes."

Level III and Conclusions

This last level (which includes both what we usually call level IIB and level III, no differences being observed between the two) is the one where the necessary and sufficient conditions are finally mastered, in spite of a few inaccuracies that may occur in determining the sufficient ones. Here, first of all, are the facts:

Phi (8;8) picks up 2, 3, and 7 and proposes J or K. It takes still another one: number 9 [picks it up]. It's not J, it is G. "Sure?" Or K or D. He eliminates F, C, B, A, J, L, and I: It could be K, D, or G. He picks up 14: It's G. "That's sufficient?" He lifts 12. I am absolutely sure that it's G. "It does not take anything else?" It should take 14 [does it]. Now, I am absolutely, absolutely sure. "A boy told me that one has to take them all off." No, with that, it's enough to be sure.

Fra (9;7), after 2, 3, and 6: It could be B, C, D, G, H, L, K [forgets F]. "Are there any that it can't be?" Yes: the A, E, I, J. I'll pick up number 7 to see if it's one that goes down straight or one that is round. He in fact removes 15. It's G. No, I have some doubt. K is similar, it's not B, H, L, it could be K, G, C, D. After 7 and 13: So, now it's between G and D; then he removes 9 for the corner and thus identifies G: It cannot be another. "You don't have to check all the boxes to be sure?" No, for example, the 6 tells me if it's round or straight.

Sab (9;11), at the end: "Open them all?" No, one doesn't have to take them all off because one can know it after seeing only a part. "How did you do it?" At first, randomly [6], and after that the number 8 to know if it's straight, round or a beak; and the 18 to know if it's pointed or not, and the 19 to see if it's straight or not.

Lip (9;10), after 9, 18, 15, 8, and 12: "One needs to open all of them?" No, *that's wrong, one can tell from just that.* "How did you do it?" *I looked around the sides.*

Flo (10;10) picks up 6, 13, 14, 8, and 19, explaining each time what she is looking for. When she has picked up an uninformative piece, she says: *That one* [3] *doesn't tell me anything new, because they're all pointed.* To remove all the covers, *that isn't worth it.* "Only small pieces?" *Yes, that's enough.* "How did you do it?" *More near the edges, because in the middle there isn't much.* "You could have done it some other way?" *I would have started there* [18–19].

Eri (11;9), after 3, 9, 5, 11, and 15: "Not all of them?" *It's not necessary: only basing oneself on the principal one, it's enough to say that it's that one or that one and, after that, one is sure that it's* G.

Aut (12;9), after only 6, 18, 12, and 16: *One can be sure.* "How?" *I took the parts where it's not the same in the others. By opening 18, one knows what it is like,* etc.

We see the unanimity of these responses in asserting the sufficiency of the necessity of G. This is in contrast to the approximate character of necessity found at level II, where subjects affirmed readily, as Tie did, that "you never know" and it's better to see all. The first question to ask is how this kind of necessity is acquired; the second question is why subjects find it sufficient.

Concerning the first point, necessity is assured by the method employed. The latter is already partially used at level II. It often remains implicit, even at level III, but the subject Fra exposes it plainly. It consists in first noting one or two clues and then constructing two complementary classes: those that are possible, or compatible with the clues identified; and those that are impossible, not possessing the characteristics in question. In this way, after having picked up 2, 3, and 6 and learning about the existence of a long tip at the top and about the beginning of a curved line in 6, Fra concludes that *B, C, D, G, H, L,* and *K* are possible (he only forgets *F*). It follows then that the class of impossible figures consists of *A, E, I,* and *J.* Following this, the clues furnished by square 15 (rectangle in the lower right) exclude *B, H,* and *L* and reduce the class of possible clues to *K, G, C,* and *D.* Then, after squares 7 and 13, there are only *G* and *D* left, and square 9 confirms *G.* Thus, necessity is the result of a top-down procedure that, at each step, diminishes the number of possibilities and correlatively increases the number of impossible choices: at the end of this iterated, systematically applied dichotomy, the figure *G* becomes necessary, being the only one possible.

The sufficient character of this method and the necessary conditions it reveals in a stepwise manner are, in contrast, the result of a process that one might qualify as bottom-up or retroactive. Once the information provided by a clue is registered, it is combined with information received previously, and one makes sure that all important aspects have been explored: "basing oneself on the principal [clue]" as Eri says, is sufficient for saying that it's this one or that one. Now this retroactive, bottom-up procedure is nothing other than integration, the condition as well as the result of necessity. It consists in uniting in one whole the various similarities and differences that are revealed by the comparison between the 12 stimulus figures and deriving from this decisions about which further areas of the large, hidden figure are still to be explored. In a word, integration is a functional mechanism, the structural expression of which is necessity.

In general, we note a regularity in the acquisitions from one level to the next. At level IA, integration is at a minimum, so that only the upper portion of the grid is explored and the successive statements are characterized by forgetting and even contradictions. The subjective certainties obtained in this way derive from a mixture of prenecessity (locally correct, but incomplete inferences) and of pseudonecessity (momentary belief that a particular choice is the only valid one, whereas, in fact, it is only one among other possible ones). At level IB, there is a beginning of integration and of local necessities, with partial exploration of both the lower and the upper portion of the grid. At level II, there is substantial progress in the order of removing covers, in the formulation of differentiated goals, and in anticipating possible clues that may yield useful information. Hence, subjects begin to constitute classes of possible and excluded figures. But the deficiency that remains is the failure to recognize exhaustivity, which prevents subjects from considering their proofs as sufficient even when they are. Only at level III does progress in integration lead to the conviction that the conditions established as being necessary, when taken together, are also sufficient.

Section II: The Necessary and Sufficient in a Problem of Possibilities

The problem studied here appears at first sight much simpler than the preceding one, since it does not involve several variables. We present subjects with two envelopes, A and B, containing respectively 10 blue chips and 5 blue plus 5 white ones. The task is then to identify the envelope from which a specified number of chips were drawn. If the subject says that one has to take out 10, we ask if with 8 or 9 one could know it too. If she says that with 6 one could already be sure, we ask if this certainty would be greater if 7 or 8, etc., chips were shown. Now, unlike the problem of the hidden figure to be reconstructed, this problem is solved by more than half of the subjects only between 10–12 years of age (level III at its usual age levels). Even at that level, only two-thirds or 8 out of 12 succeed. It seems relevant to see why the sufficiency of the conditions of an apparently obvious necessity is so late an acquisition.

Levels I and II

The following is an example of level I: Fra (6;5): "Which envelope is this?" *That with the blue chips.* "Sure?" *Don't know.* "What to do?" *Look.* "Take as many chips as you wish. How many does it take to be sure?" *Ten.* "Sure with 10?" *Yes.* "And if you took 9?" *That's not enough.* "Another child told me 6." *That's wrong.* "Why?" . . .

At this initial level, the certainty of having 10 blue chips rather than 5 blue and 5 white ones is thus assured only if the chips revealed are an exact copy of the model of 10. Even 9 do not suffice, because there would not be exact correspondence (empirical pseudonecessity).

At level II, we find a beginning of a necessitating deduction: any number of blue chips affords a beginning of certainty; but the greater the number shown, the greater the degree of certainty. Then, between IIA and IIB, subjects fix a limit below which the information becomes insufficient:

Pan (7;5): "How many does it take?" *Two.* "Sure they're all blue?" *Not very.* "So?" *More sure with 3.* "And to be completely sure?" *Four.* "Absolutely sure?" *No.* "So, how many?" *Ten, and even 9 or 8.*

Sca (8;6): "How many?" *Ten.* "Could you be sure with less?" . . . The fewest possible to be sure?" *Three.* "Completely sure?" *No, 5.* "Another child told me that it takes 6, and with 5 one cannot tell." *It's also enough with 5.* "And in the other envelope, what's in there?" *Five blue and 5 white ones.* "Perhaps you got out the 5 blue ones and left the 5 white ones inside?" *No, that's not possible* [the probability is, in fact, low, but evidently this is not how Sca reasons]. "One wouldn't be safer with 6?" *No!* [energetically]. "And 4 is not enough?" *No.* "Why? . . . And with 5 and 8, one is equally sure?" *Yes.*

Ran (9;2) pulls out 4: "That's enough to be sure?" *No, it takes 8.* "Is it better to take 8 or 10?" *Ten, because it is more.* "And as few as possible and still be sure?" *Five.* "That's enough?" *Yes.* "Why?" *Because it's half of 10.* "A boy told me that 5 is not enough, that it takes 6. Is he right?" *No* [pulls out 5 chips]. "Which envelope is it?" *The one with the blue.* "And the other?" *Five blue and 5 white.* "Perhaps you took the 5 blue ones from the other envelope?" *No, they're all blue.*

The different errors shown in these reactions are derived from the difficulty of reasoning exclusively about extension and of coordinating the necessary in A (= 10 blue chips) with the possible in B (5 blue + 5 white chips) or with what is contradictory with respect to B, and the sufficient for A with what is insufficient or redundant. What subjects need to understand is that 1 to 5 blue chips are both necessary for A but also possible for B, therefore not sufficient for proving A; that 6 to 10 blue chips are necessary for A and contradictory with B; but that 6 blue ones are sufficient and 7 to 10 are redundant. Now, the general obstacle that prevents these subtle distinctions is an insufficient dissociation between the extension of the whole or its parts and their intension. It has been known for some time that, at certain levels, subjects consider 10 elements taken from a collection of 50 to make a larger number than 10 elements taken from a collection of 20, as if extension were an intensional property. Analogously, to draw

3 to 5 blue chips suggests to the subject that all 10 are blue, and this is particularly true for 5 "because it's half of 10" [Ran, even at 9 years!]. But since in this case the subject forgets the composition of B, and, when she thinks of it again, understands the hypothetical, nonnecessary character of her formula (1 to 5) $\supset 10$, she goes back to the argument of the copy and concludes that the greater the number of blue chips drawn the greater the certainty that all are blue. This avoids the crucial difficulty of coordinating the necessary and sufficient with what is merely possible.

Level III

Only at age levels 10–12 do these multiple relationships become coordinated with the necessary. The following are two examples, the first one being of an intermediate level with respect to certainty (sufficiency):

Pat (10;1): "How many must be drawn to be sure?" *Six perhaps. If one takes 5, it would be wrong, because one might have taken the 5 blue chips* [of B], *and there would be some white ones there.* "Is it better with 10 [drawn], or 6?" *Ten, because one can see them all, one can make sure.* "Is it better with 6 or 8?" *Always with more, because one can be more sure.* "Six or 7?" *Seven* [for the same reason]. "Five or 6?" *Six, because one might have taken the 5 blue ones* [from B] *and left all the white ones in the envelope.*

Rav (10;4): *It takes 6. If you have 5 blue ones in your hand, one doesn't know if there are only blue chips or whether it is mixed.* "Six or 7, which is better?" *It's the same.* "Five isn't enough?" *No, if you've drawn only blue ones.*

Seeing Pat's straightforward reasoning about envelope B—that 5 blue ones are compatible with either 5 white chips or with 5 more blue ones—it is hard to understand why he does not see that 8 or 10 drawings would be redundant. The reason is that sufficient necessities require a tighter synthesis of necessities with possibilities than a simple inventory of the latter.

Concerning the relation between this problem and that of the hidden figure (section I), the latter is definitely easier because it only involves organizing intensive properties, whereas the present task requires dissociation and coordination of extension with intension. As already pointed out with reference to earlier research, these abilities are more complex. They require that a greater number of modalities be distinguished, in particular the minimally sufficient (6) and the nonnecessary sufficient (7–10) and, consequently, redundant in the sense of uninformative and superfluous.

9

A Proof with Interdependent Information

with J. Vauclair and E. Marbach

In the previous chapter, the different necessary conditions that the subject discovers are simply added one to the other but do not influence each other: a curve in one place does not imply an angle in another, for example. In the present study, which uses a method similar to the game Master Mind, the conditions necessary for success come from information that changes from one phase to the next, with the earlier ones having a direct impact on the later ones. There are three animal figures (a horse, H; a rabbit, R; and a chicken, C) or four ($+$a pig, P) that are hidden behind a screen and positioned in an invariant order. The child receives another set of the same objects. Her task is to place them in the same order as the experimenter's. The only information she receives in response to her moves is an indication of the number of correct positions she obtained without knowing it. This is done by means of small, yellow balls placed next to the child's row (I). The number of balls corresponds to the number of correct positions (i.e., from 0 to 3 or 4), but there is no indication as to which position is correct. The subject then builds a second row (II) under the first (I), and again we place yellow balls reflecting the number of positions identical with those of the hidden code. The subject then continues with rows III, IV, etc., one under the other.

Using these bits of partial information, which become sufficient when combined, the subject can ultimately establish the exact order. These bits of information influence each other, becoming increasingly interdependent: if everything is wrong (0 balls), the subject knows that she has to change everything, that none of the positions in rows II, III, etc., should reproduce those that were wrong and have to be eliminated once and for all. If two out of four positions are correct, the subject can infer that if she changes everything she would introduce two new errors. In short, each new bit of information must be related to all previous ones by inferential means (and not simply additively, as in chapter 8). In particular, elimination plays as positive a part as direct deductions (among the latter, let us mention the one that predicts that if two positions are correct out of three, or three out of four, then the last one must also be correct; this inference will be given particular attention). Let us also specify that if it happens that the first solution produced is correct by chance, we naturally change the code to create a new problem.

Level IA

The characteristics of this initial level are the absence of any kind of proof procedure and even of any inferential process implicating previously received information:

Ren (4;6): With three elements, *CRH*, Ren starts out with *RCH* (row I). "Why is *C* here [in position 2]?" *Because it is heavy.* "Why did I put down a ball?" *Because there is only one that's correct* "Which?" *The* R. "Are you sure?" *Yes.* "Why?" *Because I think so.* "It can't be the *C* or the *H*?" *No, no.* Row II, *HRC*: "Why *R* in the middle?" *Because he's bigger*, etc. Row III, *HCR*: "Why no ball?" *Because nothing is right.* Row IV, *CHR*, one ball: *It's because there is one right.* "Which one?" *The* R *in position 3.* "Why?" *Because it's the same in row III* [where there is nothing correct!]. Before this, Ren had been given four elements (code *HCPR*). He produces the following 11 series: *PCRH* (one correct), *PRHC*, *CPRH*, *PCRH*, *PCRH*, *PHRC*, *PRCH*, *PRCH*, *RPHC*, *RHPC*, and *PCRH*. It can be seen that Ren takes no account of the exclusions: row I, where only one is correct, is repeated without modification in rows IV and V, then in XI; similarly, row VII, where all are wrong, is repeated in VIII. In row XI, Ren declares: *I want a ball because I want the same thing as the first time*: one ball was his optimal solution.

Pat (4;11) for *HRC* gives *RHC* (one ball), then four times in a row gives *RCH*, in spite of the zero-solution on the first. Then: *I thought of putting the* H *on 3*, which gives *CRH*. But: *I want to do* RCH *again*, and she claims three balls for this regularity!

Dia (5;3) for *HRC* gives *HCR*, thus one ball, and believes it is *C* that is right; hence, in row II she gives *HCR*, again designating *C* as correct. Then she tries (III) *HRC*, which is correct by chance. "How many balls do you think you'll have?" *Two* [she does not see that if two are correct, then the third one must be correct as well]. In addition, she goes on to (IV) *RHC*, not concluding that if two are correct in row III, changing everything leads to two errors in IV.

Sam (5;4) for *HCR* gives (I) *RCH*, which he corrects immediately to (II) *RHC*, saying: R *is a bit lighter than the others*, as if expecting a seriation. He goes on in the same manner, invoking weight, and gives six rows; each gets one ball except for (II), *CRH*, which he nevertheless reproduces in IV.

Eve (6;11) for *HCR* gives seven rows of which the last is correct with help: (I) *RCH*, (II) *CHR*, (III) *HRC*, (IV) *RHC*, (V) *HRC*, (VI) *CRH*, and (VIII) *HCR*.

But for II, she still says that *R* has to be in position 3 *because he is smaller*. But in III she puts *R* in position 2 *because he already has two balls* [=one in I and one in II, even though in I *R* is in first position and in II it moves to third!]. Still, she uses a valid argument, which applies in several cases: *I did not put it in the same place before*. However, this does not prevent her from reproducing in row V an exact replica of III. In row IV, *R* is put in first position *because in III* [one ball] *he was already in I*. Similarly for *C* in position 3 *because it was there before in III and in IV*, without realizing that in IV everything is wrong (the third ball always visible!). The success in row VII is the result of chance, but it can also be explained by the fact that I–III and V are removed from the board and that only IV, VI, and VII remain visible—that is, two completely wrong ones and the correct one. Eve concludes from this, and rightly so, that *R* can only be in third position (since it is in first and in second in rows IV and VI respectively), but then immediately weakens her first deductive argument (which leads on to the next level) by denying that all is wrong in IV: *No*. Thus, all she did was to *do differently* than in rows IV and VI, following one of her two principles. The other one is the opposite—namely, to conserve a position she considered (arbitrarily) correct.

Level IA, as was true in chapter 8, shows the difficulties subjects have with proofs. Two systematic errors that are observed here can be found even in advanced age levels. Error I consists in retaining only positions 3 or 4 of a totally wrong row (zero balls) that should be excluded in all subsequent rows; and error II consists in not realizing that if a row contains one or two correct positions (even though unidentified), then changing *all* positions leads ipso facto to one or two errors. Error I is naturally the most frequent at this level. Ren, for example, constantly repeats positions copied from zero-correct rows or repeats these without modifications, such as VII repeated in VIII. Pat repeats *RCH* (zero) four times in a row. We observe error II in Dia, who attributes two balls to her row III and then corrects it in IV, not comprehending that this leads to two errors (nor that if two are correct in III, the third one is necessarily also correct). Aside from these two errors, christened I and II because we frequently find them again at subsequent levels, we can note as specific to this level the belief that the positions are ordered by weight (Ren and Sam) or size (Ren and Eve), which is not absurd but unverifiable. More interesting is the subjective certainty attached to certain positions that are not confirmed by anything. Ren is "sure" that *R* is first, the sole argument being "because I think so." Pat insists on repeating *RCH*, where all are wrong. Dia declares correct the center position of *C*. In all this we can discern a very instructive inability to conceive of a plurality of possibilities, which explains the absence of mental construction and the numerous contradictions.

Nevertheless, we find two rudimentary formulations of strategies, pronounced in Eve, that may appear contradictory but that are valid as a compromise. They become increasingly important at later levels, when they can be based on legitimate inferences. But in the primitive form in which Eve announces them, these indications correspond to certain reactions already found in the subjects just presented, although we are still far removed from any kind of method. The first of these incomplete formulations consists in saying "I did not put it in the same place before," which amounts to saying that in case of zero or one ball, one should permute the items in some way. This is effectively what happens in many cases and is, in fact, necessary. The second formulation, which is usually applied erroneously at this level but which later on will provide useful probability clues, is [I put *x* on *n*] because it was there before [in a previous row]." Subjects at more advanced levels will say that if *x* is found at the same place in several rows, with one ball, the chances are that it is correct. But subjects at this level are still far from such subtleties. They content themselves, as does Eve, with simply repeating positions that they subjectively consider valid.

Level IB

The important progress that characterizes this second phase is the replacement of subjective certainty by the awareness and formulation of *perhaps* – in other words, by an opening toward other possibilities.

Fre (6;2) for *RCH* first gives (I) *CRH*: "How many balls?" *Perhaps three correct, perhaps two, perhaps one.* "And perhaps 0?" *Yes.* "It is one." *Maybe the* C . . . *or the* H. He does row II: *HCR*. "Explain?" *I did the opposite, I've moved them a bit.* "How many balls?" *Two, for* C *and* R. *Maybe the* R *was not right* [in *I*] *and maybe the* H *was right.* "That gives a ball?" *Maybe it's the* C *or the* H. "And the *R*?" *That too.* He does row III: *RHC*. "Why C in third position?" *Because if I put it in 1, that gives the same as in I, and if I put it in 2, that's like in II.* The same reasoning for *H.* "How many balls?" *Three, two, or one.* "That gives one. Where will you put *H* in the next row?" *I don't know yet.* He puts up (IV) *HCR*, (VI) *HCR*, and (VII) *RCH*. "There [VI], you already had something like that?" *Yes, there* [II]. *I would always put the same thing so it would be everywhere* [points to all the rows]; *one could also do the opposite of IV.* As for VII, he says: *because it's perhaps* H *or* C *that is correct in II* [and which nevertheless he inverts in relation to *R*]. At 5;10, Fre had already been interviewed with four elements, *HCPR*. He had given (I) *PRHC*, (II) *HCRP*, (III) *CPHR*, (IV) *RHCP*, (V) *RHCP*, (VI) *CPRH*, and (VII) *HCPR*. Since (V) yielded zero balls, he concluded: *So that means that* P *was not right in row II.* Thus we see that he found the solution in VIII by retaining II and interchanging *R* and *P*.

Nil (6;6), with *CHR*, begins with (I) *HRC* (zero). He corrects to (II) *RHC* and (III) *CHR* (which is correct): "Why did you not leave *C* in position 3?" *Because C on 3 is wrong here* [I], *so I put it like that.* "Do you think that everything is right now?" *I don't see how one can tell if it's right: I just put it like that.* He then adds (IV) *RCH*, which also modifies row I. We change the code: *RCH*. He gives (I) *HCR* (one correct), then (II) *CRH* (*H* correct), saying: *There* [I], *there was already an* H, *the 2, I probably shouldn't change that.* He goes on to (III) *CHR*: "None right." *The* R *should then go in the middle.* (IV) *RHC*: "How was it in III?" *None right: here* [IV], *the* H *is in the middle, too. That's not right, so* C *should go in the middle and* H *to* 3. (V) *RCH* (correct): "That seems correct to you now? *Yes.* "Could it be some other way?" *That I don't know. It's quite possible. But I just do not know.* He tries (VI) *HRC*. "More like row V or VI?" *Row VI seems more correct.* "Why?" *I don't really know.* "But V, is it possible?" *Yes.* But no reason is given.

Bea (6;6), with *HRC*: After (I) *HCR*, she is lucky to have (II) *CHR*, where all are wrong and (after III, *RHC*) to rearrange a row (IV, *RCH*) where nothing is correct either: from rows II to IV she could, thus, deduce the correct sequence with certainty. She first seems to move in that direction by putting up (V) *HRC*, saying: *There isn't yet an* R *in this spot* [2, after having looked at I and II]; and *the* C, *I've only put it twice: it's perhaps the* C *that's right in row V.* We then ask her what zero balls means in II and IV. *That means that they are all in the wrong places.* But when asked: "If you look at rows II and IV again, can you tell which animal is surely in the wrong place?" She still answers: *Perhaps the* R. "Why?" *Don't know.* She then puts up (VI) *RHC* and expects *maybe three balls.* "No, one." *Perhaps it's the* C *that's right,* hence the interchange *HRC*, which is correct, but without justification.

Vin (7;3), with *HCR*, is as lucky as Bea: After row I (*RCH*=one ball), he builds two wrong rows (II) *RHC* and (III) *CRH*. But he only repeats *RCH* (IV =I) and then finds the correct solution in V, his only argument being: *I've changed the animals' places.* "Changed from what?" *From row III.* "Only from III?" *Yes, only from III.* "You don't forget that there was zero for II?" *Yes.* "So, this row V [*HCR*], how did you do it?" *I've done it differently from IV.* "You looked at what when you decided to place *R*, for example?" *I looked at row IV because if I were looking at* R *in 1 it would be the same thing.* Vin recognizes that *R* in position 1 (I) had turned out to be wrongly placed, given II. "And the *C* in row V, is it also in the wrong place?" *I don't know. But if the* R *was wrong in row II, I cannot change it against the* H *in row V. If the* H *was right in row I, the* R *must go back to 1, so that doesn't work.* "So?" *We leave it like that* [V], but without being certain.

Ani (7;6), with *HCR*, gives (I) *CHR* (1 ball), then (II) *RHC*: *I thought it was the* H *that's right, so I changed places* [permuting *R* with *C*]. "It's zero." *They're all wrong.* Then (III) *CRH* (another zero), and from there (IV) *HCR* (correct). *Here* [III], *it was wrong, so I had to turn them all around.* "Is there another way to get it right?" *This one* [(V) *HRC*]. "Which of the two do you prefer [IV or V]?" *This one* [IV]. "Why?" *Don't know.* "Is it possible to know?" *No.*

Sop (7;6), with four elements *RCHP*, begins with (I) *RHPC*, then does (II) *RHCP*, and, continuing to permute *C, H,* and *P,* finds (III) *RCHP* (correct). But instead of giving four balls, we only put up three; she does not see that three correct implies the fourth, and she corrects to (IV) *PRCH*, which she declares *just as correct* as row III, whereas not a single position is the same in the two series.

These many examples are highly informative from the point of view of inference. The important progress the subjects show is their openness to various possibilities. Positions and number of correct choices are always proposed with some openness to doubt as one possibility. The general principle underlying these reactions is well formulated by Nil: "I don't see how one can tell if it's right." But what subjects do not as yet comprehend — except for unusual cases, and then only partially — is that it is, however, possible to know what is wrong and that by making use of and composing the excluded cases one finds the correct solution. In particular, they do not see that two completely wrong rows allow one to infer the correct solution with necessity. For example, Nil, who produced two zero rows (I and III), corrects III by moving *H*, which is wrong in III, and thus finds the correct row V; but he still believes another row, VI, to be also possible, a row already contradicted by row I, even considering that row VI "seems more correct." Bea may well say that the fact that II and IV give zero is because "they are all in the wrong places," but she identifies only *R* as being placed wrongly, and even adds "perhaps." Vin gives two wrong rows, II and III, and limits himself to taking account of III only for changing "the animals' places." Ani, after rows II and III (zeros), finds IV correct because "here [III] it was wrong, so I have to turn them all around," but still believes that V too can be right and affirms that one cannot be sure whether IV or V is more correct. Sop believes row IV " just as correct as III, two rows that have not a single element in common.

In short, these subjects do not yet coordinate the excluded cases in any systematic fashion. They only use them locally, in isolated instances. Aside from this, the procedures used are the ones that began to be developed at level IA: do "the opposite," as Fre said, in the case of a failure; or judge the correctness of a position by its frequency (sufficient or insufficient): Bea places a *C* because she has "only put it twice," or an *R* because "there isn't yet [one] in ths spot [position 2]." Fre applies this second method to the point where it amounts to tautological repetitions: he reproduces previous rows, saying: "I would always put the same thing so it would be everywhere," as if frequency as such (including wrong choices) could make things right.

Level II

With the development of concrete operations, we observe in children from 7-8 and 10-11 years of age a marked progress in the use of inferred necessity. Exclusions are now used to a greater or lesser extent, but coordination is not yet complete:

Syl (7;2), with *HCR*, puts up (I) *RHC*, expecting to obtain two correct ones for *C* and *H*, without seeing that in that case the third one is necessarily correct. We tell her that it is zero, and she modifies three positions (and not two) to get (II) *CRH*, specifying that she has changed everything. "Could you have done it differently?" *Yes*, [III] HCR, which we ignore for the moment. "How many balls for row II?" *Two or three.* "It's zero. . . . So?" *So, it's what I have put up in row III.* "How many for III?" *Three balls.* "Are you sure?" *Yes.* "Why?" *Because it's zero in I and in II.* "Could one do it differently to have three balls?" *No.* We suggest IV = *CHR*, and she gives in for a moment but then says that *C* is not *correct in IV . . . because it was not right in II.*

Rol (8;5), with *HCR*, gives *RCH*, receives a ball, and then does (II) *CRH*: *because maybe it was that one* [H] *that was correct in row I.* "*No ball.*" *I'll have to do it over.* (III) = *RHC*. "No ball." (IV) = *CHR*: *because perhaps the H was right before* [in III!]. "How many balls in III?" . . . She changes IV to V [*RCH*]. "Why H in position 3?" *It has to go to 1 because it hasn't been there yet.* She then puts up *HCR* (correct) *because in row III there is a C and that was wrong, and in row II, R is wrong.* Thus she finally makes use of exclusions imposed by II and III at once.

Tri (8;5), with *RCH*, gives (I) *CRH* (1 ball), (II) *HRC* (zero), and (V) *RCH* (correct). After III, we ask: "Does it help to look at the rows where there are yellow balls [which he interprets as "look at the preceding rows"]?" *Yes, in row II, it was all wrong, so that allowed me to change.* "And what if there is one ball?" *Yes. . . . Perhaps not. Yes, alright, but one cannot tell which one is right, so that doesn't help.* After row IV, he indicates that *I knew that C on 3 was wrong* [in II], *and the H, I know now that it's wrong on 2 because in row IV there is no ball*: hence (V).

Sim (8;10), with *RCH*, makes (I) *CRH*, with unjustified certainty concerning the correct element. But after (II) *CHR* and (III) *HRC*, both wrong, she draws the conclusion (V) *RCH* (correct): *because here* [II and III], C *was always wrong and the R was wrong, I believe.* "How many balls do you expect?" *Three.* "Sure?" *Yes.* With a new code, *HCR*, she gives (I) *RCH* (1 ball), then (II) *CHR*, but says immediately, *No, that's wrong: I haven't used one the same* [as in I], which means that she did not commit error II (defined above): if there is one ball (i.e., one correct choice), changing all three amounts to committing at least one error.

Dio (9;4) with *RHC*, gives (I) *HCR* (zero) and concludes *RHC* (correct) from that, based on the principle that everything has to be changed; but he recognizes that his order could not be demonstrated in comparison with *CRH*. However, he accepts that *R* could be in position 3, which is contradictory with respect to the wrong row I (errorI). Given a new code, *RCH*, he obtains two zero rows from which he infers the correct one by means of completely explicit reasons, encountered for the first time so far in our interviews: *I'll put* R *on 7 because there* [in I], *it was on 3 and that was wrong, and because in row II it was wrong in position 2.* "And the others?" *I put* C *on 2 because in row I it was on 1 and that was wrong, and in row II it was on 3*, etc., for *H*.

Jul (9;6), with *CRH*, engages in a series of more or less systematic permutations: *HRC→HCR→CHR*, moving *C* from position 3 to 2 and to 1 while conserving *HR*; then *RCH* and *RHC*, but since two of these five rows give zero, she infers the correct row as the preceding subjects did.

Ala (9;7), similarly: *I keep one animal in the place, and I cross the two others: CRP→PRC→CPR*, etc.

It is not surprising to find that, with four elements, the reactions are at a lower level:

Eti (8;6), with *PCHR*, gives (I) *RHCP* (zero). He then corrects to (II) *PCRH* (two balls), having changed all positions, and in (III) *HRPC* (zero) does not retain any of the positions in (II), thus committing error II−except for conserving the pair *PC*, which may be by chance. Then (IV) *CPRH* (two balls) is followed by (V) *PHRC* (one ball), where *H* in position 2 is excluded by row I and *C* in 4 by III (two instances of error I); in VI, he puts up *CPHR* (two balls), followed by (VII) *PCRH* (two balls), where nothing remains of (VI) (error II); VIII gives *RHPC*, where *C* on 4 is excluded by row III; finally, row IX is correct with recourse to some exclusions.

Cat (9;1), with *HPCR*, gives (I) *CRHP* (zero), followed by (II) *RPCH* (two balls). Then row III is *CPRH*, which conserves *P* in position 2 and *H* in 4 (no error I), but contains *C* in 1, which is excluded by row I.

San (10;3) produces nine rows, avoiding two instances of errors II out of three possible; but she retains in three different rows, three positions excluded by three null series (zero rows). However, she obtains in row X the correct solution based on the exclusions imposed by these null series and on the agreements seen in the rows with two balls.

Considerable progress is made at this level (with three elements) in the sense of correct anticipations, with reasons given and based on excluded choices (see particularly Dio) and on exploratory strategies (Jul and Ala). Nevertheless, the coordinations are not always complete between the positions chosen and the exclusions, and they are even less so with four elements. However, with three elements and in the case of two or more null series, subjects take into account their constellations and not only the immediately preceding one, as is the case at level IB. Error I (forgetting exclusions), however, is more persistent than error II (changing all positions in the case of one or two balls), particularly with four elements. On the other hand, none of these subjects understands as yet that if three out of four positions are correct, the fourth one is necessarily correct also.

Level III

With the onset of hypothetico-deductive operations, it is not surprising that the inferential mechanisms, which were already at work at level II, are generalized at level III:

Mar (10;4), with *HRC*, gives (I) *HCR* (one ball), then (II) *CHR*: "Zero." *Good!* "Does that annoy you?" *No, no, it's either* H *or* C *that is correct in row* I *[R in 3 being excluded by II]. Perhaps, I'll decide* [=suppose] *that it's* H *and so I have to invert* C *and* R *of the first combination* [I]: *it's* [III] HRC *[correct].* "How many balls does this get you?" *One or three. It can't be two, because if there are two, the third one is necessarily correct, also. . . . But I could have another possibility* [IV] RCH *[compatible with row I and not contradictory with II] to see whether it is* C *that is right in row I.*

And *(11;0), with PCR, gives* (I) *RPC.* "Zero." *I will have to change everything:* (II) *PCR* (correct). We give him two balls only, but he protests immediately: *That seems to me a bit impossible: if there are two correct, well, the third one, I can't move it.* We correct to three balls. New code: *PRC.* He puts up *CPR.* "That's zero. Does that bother you?" *No, I don't mind.* (III) *RCP:* "Zero." He puts up *PRC. I think that this time it's right* [sure].

Ano (11;6), after two null series and a correct solution, is given a new problem: the possibility of three different animals or two identical ones, the hidden code being *CCP.* She puts up (I) *PCR* (one ball), (II) *PRC* (zero), (III) *RCP* (two balls), (IV) *RCR* (one ball), and (V) *CCP*, which is judged correct. We ask if there is another possibility, and she tries (VI) *RPP.* "That would do?" *Ah! no, that wouldn't do because in row I there was one ball for* PCR *and, in row VI, it's not that at all.* In other words, we have here a case of avoiding error II in a new situation where it was not easy to think of it.

Isa (10;3), with four elements (*HCPR*), puts up first (I) *HPRC* (one ball), then (II) *CPHR*, specifying that she can only keep one element of row I without knowing which one. For row III, she announces: *I shall put some in the same places as in row II to know which ones were right.* She retains *R* in position 4 (as in row II) and *H* in 1 (as in I), thus: *HCPR. I've guessed a bit, I didn't have proof yet.* We offer three balls, which she accepts at first, then: *That's impossible: it's either two or four.* We give her four. We tell her that, in the new code, there may be an element that gets repeated. Basing herself on the exclusions from two null series and on three others with one ball, she achieves (V) *CHRP.* We give her three balls, specifying that this time it is really three: she corrects to *CHHP* (correct).

We see not only that eliminations become systematic, but also that subjects immediately know how to use a null series (Mar and And). Error I has finally disappeared, and error II is avoided by Ano even in the more difficult series with repeated elements. Progress can also be observed in the use of co-possibilities, as was already evident at level IB with the "perhaps" that subjects used in their first explorations. But at level III, when, for example, Mar finds a correct solution that cannot be proved, there remains "another possibility that is not contradicted by the preceding row.

One interesting indication of the generality of deductive processes is subjects' refusal to accept two out of three or three out of four correct positions, because the last one is "necessarily correct" in that case (Mar, etc.). Vin, at level IB when told that he had two (out of three) correct, said of the third piece that "one should leave it like that" because information about two positions precludes the choice of the third; but for all that, he did not consider the third piece as correct. And, who also said of the third one that "I cannot move it," concludes from this that it must be correct and that two out of three correct, "that seems to me a bit impossible," which is a polite way of telling the experimenter that she is not being serious.

Conclusions

This research has dealt with a form of necessity that is essentially negative, of the kind "if, out of n possibilities, $n \times 1$ are to be excluded, then the nth is necessary." Since the order of elements in the hidden code is arbitrary, there is no *positive* criterion that can be invoked in trying to rebuild the series. The only information available is either that all positions are to be eliminated, in the case of a null series, or that one or two choices are correct but without any indication which they are. Nevertheless, such negative or partially positive information permits rigorous deduction if all positions of a null series are definitely excluded and if not every position in a partially correct series is changed—that is, if what we have been calling *error I* and *error II* are avoided.

The surprising result of the preceding observations is that only at level III, at 11–12 years, are complete inferences attained. Two reasons may explain this phenomenon. The first is already familiar to us: negation or negative factors are more difficult to handle than positive ones. The second is specific to this research: a negative term is generally in opposition to a positive, observable one—this glass is partially empty, because it is not full; not all flowers are primroses, because there are daisies; etc. But in the present situation a null series is not to be *discarded* in favor of an actual, positive one, but is to be *conserved* to the end so that a positive use can be made of it, but in a deductive manner.

The persistence of error I, as opposed to error II, can be explained not only in terms of the greater difficulty of conserving exclusions until the end (i.e., at longer intervals): thus, Ano corrects row VI because it contains none of the positions of row I, in which one was correct. But the main explanation is more likely to be the greater difficulty of conserving exclusions as opposed to partially correct solutions, even if their content is unknown.

A second interesting aspect of this research is the optimal example it presents of the connection between possibility and necessity. Since the information received only concerns what is possible or impossible, deductive inference amounts to relating the two, progressively reducing the domain of possibilities until the necessary imposes itself as the only possibility. This teaches us something about the nature of necessity itself.

10

A Case of a Necessary Limit

Young subjects notice early on that the number of permutations that can be carried out on an ordered series of objects increases with the number of elements in the series, and this happens long before the developmentally late discovery of the law $n!$ that determines this number. It seemed to us instructive, from the point of view of necessity, to ask children between 5 and 13–14 years of age to perform such permutations on two and then on three objects and to explain why, in the latter case, the maximum number of different permutations is necessarily six. It is interesting to see how a subject justifies this necessary limitation, which has to do with impossibility or (put differently) with a somehow negative necessity, as opposed to those that apply in the case of logico-mathematical, additive, and multiplicative conservations.

The method we use is very simple. We ask subjects to draw first two, then three crosses of different colors (XXX), and then to change their linear order (for example, blue B, green G, and red R), creating a vertical array of as many different rows as they can think of. If a subject stops too soon, we propose a different sequence and see if she can add another. If she succeeds in continuing and, especially, if she gets the six possible ones, we ask the same questions; if she declines to go beyond six, the main problem is to explain why there cannot be more.

Levels IA and IB

Subjects at level IA content themselves with one or two permutations, or they add simple repetitions of sequences already produced without seeing that they are repetitions:

Ced (5;7) gives RGB, then BGR. "Another one?" Repeats RGB. "You haven't done that one yet?" *No.* "And that one [row 1]?" *Oh, yes.* "Can you do another one?" *No.* "It's impossible?" *With more colors, yes.* We start over with a different set: he only finds BGR and GRB.

Ern (5;5), with *B* and *R* gives *BR* and *RB*, twice. "Why are *BR* and *RB* not the same?" *I don't know.* With three colors, he does *BGR* and *GBR* twice, again *BGR, BRG*, and again *GBR*. He does not find any others and cannot explain the nature of the differences.

Mar (5;10) only finds three different sequences and repeats her first in the fourth row. "The last one is new?" *Yes, it is different from that one* [row 1, the same sequence]. "Why?" She points to the shape of the elements: × instead of +.

What is noteworthy about these reactions is how little subjects become conscious of order relations, and therefore of the problem presented: Ced does not see that his fourth row is a reproduction of his first; Ern and Mar, similarly, do not notice other identical sequences. Ern cannot explain the difference between *BR* and *RB*, and Mar sees the dissimilarity only in the shape of the crosses and not in their sequence. The result is that subjects discover few possibilities.

At level IB, subjects just begin to give consideration to positional relationships:

Car (5;6) comes up with four different orders, but then repeats one of them. She ends with *BGR* and *BRG*, saying: *Oh, I am stupid:* B *is the same, but* GR *and* RG, *that's not the same.*

Ant (6;8) produces only three different orders, considering these the only possible ones *because we've put the green one here, the blue one there, and the red there. On that one, we've put the blue one first, the red one there* . . . [she enumerates each position produced]. On the next trial, she produces again three orders without noticing that these are different ones from those she produced in trial 1.

Dia (6;4) finds four different sequences by first varying the initial element *B*, then *R* and *G*; after that, she puts *R* in the initial position and permutes *B* and *G*. "How did you find that?" *Because the colors are mixed up;* R *is there, then there, then there: the same thing with* B *and* G. *They change places.* We start over, and this time she only finds three different sequences: "Are there still others?" *I found them all.* "I believe that if you start with *G*, you can still do something different." *Oh, yes* [permutes *B* and *R* and finds the six]. *I put the* B *in first place because it has never been first,* etc.

Rik (6;9) also finds only four sequences, and, given the same suggestion by the experimenter, she likewise completes six. But to justify that there are no more, she merely says: *because they're already all made.*

Nic (7;3) begins with a promising remark: *I can't do the same things the same places,* but later he considers wrong the series *GRB* because the first was *BRG* and *R* remains in the center. Once he understands that one can also change only one or two positions, he says that in that case *it's easy.* . . . *One can do many* . . . *thousands! One can do that color, then that color, then that color,* . . . etc. *One can do a whole lot.* In fact, he manages only four, then five, and, starting over, comes up twice with three series. *I think there are only six.* "Explain to me why only six?" *I shall try to do seven.*

The task for these subjects is to have the elements "change places," as Dia and Nic say. But they do not yet understand that linear order is a variable that can be transformed in a systematic way by means of ordered permutations. In other words, they do not yet use any strategy to carry out permutations, but proceed by simple trial-and-error methods. If aided by some suggestions, however, they can complete their series and come to find all six permutations. But it is clear that they in no way understand why six is the maximum. Rik contents herself with thinking that those are the only possible ones because they're "already all made," and Nic, who says the same thing, nevertheless proposes to "try to do seven," after having believed in an infinite number.

Levels II and III

From 7–8 years on, one finds subjects who succeed in finding the six possibilities by going somewhat beyond simple empirical explorations, using rudimentary strategies that, however, are still only local and without generality:

Ser (7;6), after a few empirical attempts, places each of the three elements first and completes the rest by permuting the two remaining ones: *First,* B *was in first position, then* G *was first, and after that,* R *was first.* He states that all are done, but without justification.

Jer (7;11) systematically permutes the first with the last: *I've done the opposite of that one,* then modifies the position of all the others. "Are there others aside from the *G?*" *Don't know.*

Isa (8;3), after a few explorations, puts *GRB* underneath *RGB* and completes the three series with one of the three elements in first position by permuting the remaining two elements. But while saying that, in this way, she has *already all,* the only reason she gives is that *I cannot find any more.* More importantly, with three other colors she cannot predict the same number of six series: *I don't know, one has to try.*

Top (9;7) similarly completes six series: *I've done all the possibilities. I started the same way and then I changed the two others around. Then I tried to do the same with the last one, but I saw that I already did those.* "One could start in the middle?" *Yes.* "There will be more than six?" *Yes.* "Try." *No, it can't be done.* "Why?" *Because if one changes the others around, it's already done.*

Cri (9;9) first finds five series and considers six or seven *impossible.* Then he gets six: *I've only switched them around. In the first row,* B *was in the middle, the second, too; but* R, *I've put it first and* G *last,* etc. He gives all the details of what he did. "Very good, There are no others?" *No, I can't seem to find any more* [tries]. *I'll see if I can do another one still* [cannot]. "Do you think I could?" *I have no idea.*

Pat (9;3) rapidly completes the series of six. "Do you think you have found them all?" *Yes.* "How do you know?" *There are three colors, and one can only change those three.* "That makes how many?" *Six.* "Why? . . . Did you follow a particular order?" *No. I looked at what I did, and if I hadn't done it, then I did it.* "How?" *There are only six possibilities, so I try to find six.* "Why 6 rather than 4 or 10? . . . "

Jan (10;6) completes six series on a single try. *I've got them all.* "Another one still?" *No, there are no more colors: with three, I found everything.* "And me, I might find seven?" *Perhaps.*

Interestingly, these subjects discover a more or less exhaustive procedure and are able to describe it, without, however, succeeding in justifying that six series constitute a *maximum.* Having stated that she cannot get any other possibilities, Isa is even unable to predict that with three other colors one would find the same limit of six. In other words, this limit of six is not yet seen as necessary. For these subjects it is nothing more than an expression of what they have been able to obtain with their actions, without being sure that the adult might not achieve more.

At level III, however, the limit of six becomes the necessary consequence of the operations involved—that is, of the type and number of possible inversions:

Ana (10;11) immediately constructs the whole series. "There aren't any others?" *No.* "Why?" *Because I have the same color twice in first place* and, each time, *I put the last color first.* This amounts to saying that the two kinds of inversion, those between extremes and those between contiguous elements, exhaust all possibilities.

Ced (11;6), following an immediate success, similarly says that he is certain that there are no more than six possibilities because *I've put the three colors in the first column in one way, then another way in the second column, and another way in the third.* "But do you think I could do seven?" *I don't really think so.*

San (12;0): *I've done all.* "Do you think that I could get seven?" *No.* "Why?" *Because I've inverted all the colors: I've first taken* [mentally] *the G, then the R, then the B, and I've inverted the other two.*

Pac (12;9) is *absolutely certain* that there are only six series, *because all the six have been done* [=put in three different positions], *all the R have been done, and all the B have been done.* In fact, he had, in the first column, *G, R,* and *B* twice each, and then permuted the two remaining ones.

Art (13;1) uses the same system and the same arguments.

The limit of six series is here seen as being invested with necessity. This necessity is intrinsic, deriving from the relationships involved with their possible inversions. At level II the seriations are carried out without a program, whereas at level III they are applied by following an ordered sequence. This means, then, that the operations involved in permutation consist in seriations of seriations—

that is, second-power seriations. This explains their difficulty, but also the necessity of the connections.

Some of the subjects even understand the law for four colors: San, for example, says that if there are six possibilities for three, there will be $6 \times 4 = 24$ when a fourth color is added: When asked, "And if I tell you more than 24?", she replies, "That's not true, I found all of them." Similarly, another subject, 13-year-old Hut, says that, in going from three to four elements, "there is one more color that can change places with all the others," hence $4 \times 6 = 24$. Some subjects, however, regress to level II when having to deal with four elements.

We are here interested not in the construction of the law $n!$, however, but in the formation of necessity when subjects pass form a mere description of actions (level II) to the comprehension of the *reason* for their success. This comprehension begins when subjects are no longer satisfied with finding all the different seriations that they are able to distinguish, but discover that these seriations are related to one another by a law that is itself of a serial nature: "One has to follow an order," says Hut. This law imposes both the necessity of a sufficient number (six in the case of three crosses) and that of an upper limit for this number that if violated, leads to mere repetition of previous series. These two aspects characterize the particular type of necessary composition analyzed in this chapter and constitute their main interest.

Conclusions

The principal results of the present research can be summarized in the following three points: (1) Necessity pertains to the compositions carried out by the subject and is not an observable datum inherent in objects; (2) it is not an isolated and definitive state, but the result of a process (necessitation); and (3) it is directly related to the constituting of possibilities that generate differentiations, whereas necessity is related to integration—hence, the two formations are in equilibrium.

I

In considering whether necessity has an exogenous or endogenous origin, one might think of the necessity of a slope causing a marble to roll (chapter 3) as a good example of that *real necessity*, the one situated in things, that Aristotle believed existed.* If we stick to observable facts, we see only that a marble placed on a slope will "always" roll down and "never" up. But this is merely extensional generality, and therefore a law that becomes necessary only when there is a deductive model furnishing explanations. Would it be sufficient to invoke the "fall of heavy bodies"? But this is still only an observable translated into a general law. With the advent of Newtonian gravity, necessity was based on a model that proposed an explanation: "universal attraction." But this is still only disguised description, and it is only with Einstein and Misner and with Wheeler's geometrodynamics† that explanations are proposed that are more basic because they are related to the geometric operations of the subject (including possible future elaborations). True, one might say that any general fact—such as the de-

---

*Even Montesquieu, in speaking of legal norms, said: "Laws are necessary relations deriving from the nature of things," an analogous confusion between the normative and the factual.

---

†In J. A. Wheeler, *Geometrodynamics* (New York: Academic Press, 1962).

scent of marbles on a slope—appears intuitively necessary because the subject knows that there is an explanation even if she does not know what it is. However, this argument leaves the door open for pseudonecessities as well as for valid justifications.

In chapters 1 and 2, the necessity attributed to reality is the result of certain mediators (the principle of conservation in chapter 1 and subjective geometry in chapter 2). These are part of the subject's logico-mathematical structures, but they can also be applied directly to the objects (the geometry of proper motion, of material action, which pertains both to the subject and the object).

In short, necessity does not emanate from objective facts, which are by their nature merely real and of variable generality and therefore subject to necessary laws to a greater or lesser extent. They only become necessary when integrated within deductive models constructed by the subject. The necessity of p can thus not be characterized only as the impossibility of not-p, since new possibilities can always emerge, but must be described in Leibniz's manner as the contradiction of not-p, and this relative to a specific, limited model.

II

What, then, is this endogenous origin of necessity? One may start with the proverbial "Nil est sine ratione" of Leibniz, but it only characterizes the second of the three dimensions of necessity that we are going to distinguish below. Undoubtedly, a more general normative principle will have to be assumed, such as the principle of contradiction, which excludes the coexistence of p and of not-p but does not tell us whether n implies p or not-p; or the principle of sufficient reason, which does not specify what this reason is (hence the use made of it by Aristotle to rule out inertia, and by Galilei to justify it). Such a principle at the base of the necessitation process, and one having axiomatic validity, would be: "It is necessary that necessities exist," without specifying what they are. But why do there have to be necessities? It is because without them thinking would constantly contradict itself, if it retained all prior assertions, or would get lost in Heraclitean flux, if it forgot or neglected them. And since thinking is always in development it cannot do otherwise, if it is to avoid these two problems, than to integrate the past within the current state. Such integration, once complete, is the source of necessity.

But this only moves the problem one step back: where, in turn, does this need for integration come from? Two objects or events may be similar to each other, and this relation of similarity, once established, is one condition for integration. On the other hand, they may be dissimilar. Unlike similarities, however, which tend to be absolute (as in identity), dissimilarities are never complete: no matter how different two real or conceptual entities are, they still have certain analogies as empirical or cognitive objects. Inasmuch as similarities lead to assimilations and dissimilarities to accommodations, the latter relations are subordinated to the former as accommodations are to assimilations. The fact that there has to be mutual assimilation of schemata at all possible levels of their interaction then imposes a permanent need for integration, from which necessitations proceed.

Stated more simply, the assimilatory schemata cannot function in isolation. Their constant need to find new inputs must lead to coordinations, which we characterize in terms of their mutual assimilation. These compositions, and not the initial individual constitutions, ensure the integrative processes.

We thus define as necessary those processes the composition C of which cannot be negated without leading to a contradiction. It is obvious, and this confirms the role of assimilation, that only the subject's own actions (or operations) permit the verification of the contradictory nature of not-C. Reality can only indicate that not-C, in fact, never occurs, which is insufficient to demonstrate its impossibility (the latter can be disproved by modifying the conditions). In particular, the complete integration of the past within the current state, which is a condition for logico-mathematical necessity, can only be inferential in nature, as opposed to other subject activities such as the modification of habits (a new habit only retains a more or less limited portion of preceding ones).

III

Being closely allied to integration, necessity thus consists in an auto-organization *causa sui*. It is not an observable datum in the real world. It is a product of systematic compositions that involves a dynamic of necessitating processes rather than being limited to states. This dynamic begins with the formation of concepts susceptible of and designed for mutual composition. It takes its departure from situations in which the organization of concepts is heterogeneous and includes only partial comparisons in terms of similarities and differences and where coordinations by reciprocal assimilations are not attained. This has been documented in chapters 4 and 5 concerning lengths. Subjects first resort to the use of incompatible criteria: an oblique is judged "longer" than a horizontal line of the same length at one moment "because it goes up," and soon after is shorter for the same reason. We saw similar contradictions with regard to a vertical and a horizontal line, one or the other being judged "more straight"; or, with centrations on endpoints of two parallel lines at the expense of points of origin, etc. Finally, subjects come to adopt a homogeneous criterion: the interval between these two points, which makes possible the associative compositions.

The search for necessity continues as subjects come to use operational processes such as reflective abstraction and the various forms of completive generalization and, finally—the base of all inferential logic—certain fundamental operations that we have come to designate *significant implications*, in which $p \supset q$ is necessary to the extent that the meaning of q is included in that of p.

Unlike the modal logic of Lewis—in which necessity is derived by means of an additional operator, which is insufficient in resolving the problems of paradoxical implication specific to extensional logic—the logic of entailment of Anderson and Belnap takes necessity as being inherent in the operation itself if, as is the case with our significant implication, in the relation $p \supset q$, q can be deduced from p by means of natural inference.

Once these operations are acquired, the necessitating processes extend to the construction of logico-mathematical structures in which closures alternate with new openings, and further to explanatory physical models where exogenous or external variations are continually replaced by endogenous or internal ones. These variations are deducible, and their internal compositions become necessary. Both the processes of structuring and of modelization result in a need for justification that brings about new necessities. These newly acquired capacities permit the constant production of new extensions.

IV

It is possible to distinguish two different forms of necessity, one pertaining to functional stages and the other to structural *force*. From the point of view of functions, there are three main stages; these do not correspond to general, developmental stages, but to phases in the solution of a problem or in the construction of a particular model (chapters 1–3), of a structure (as with the lengths of chapter 4), or of pro-structures (the associativities of chapters 5 and 6 and the distributivity of chapter 8).

The first stage is that of *preparatory determinations*, or of the search for necessary conditions and then for necessary and sufficient conditions: this aspect of necessity has been studied particularly, in respect to the construction of proofs, in chapters 8 and 9. But one can find it in the process of the solution of any kind of problem, especially in that of the construction of slopes (chapter 3) or rotations (chapter 2).

The second stage may be designated by the term *elaboration* or *analysis*; this is the search for an explanation, A, of the necessity of a composition, followed by explanation B for A, C for B, etc., in a never-ending process. This is, without any doubt, the principal driving force in the search for necessity and the characteristic that distinguishes it best from mere extensional generalization. In fact, it is evident that the basis for the necessity of a composition (for example, in a seriation $A < B < C$ . . . $< X$, there is transitivity in the relationships $<$, and there are as many terms $> A$ as there are $< X$) is not that it is "always" correct, which remains on the level of generality without demonstration that it is necessarily so, but rather that it is based on significant implications that provide the explanation: the developmental facts clearly show the transition from extensional generality to deductive justification. This change occurs only at about 7 years of age.

The third stage toward necessity may be called *amplification*. It consists in deriving necessary consequences from a previously *necessitated* composition. This third development, which can occur a good deal later than the preceding one, can be found in the difficulty (studied in chapter 7) subjects experience in going from distributivity with conservation of the initial whole (the tasks *CT* and *ST*) to the other, where the whole is altogether divided (the tasks *BT* and *LT*), even though the latter is only a consequence of the former. In the domain of the history of science, this phenomenon is relatively frequent. For example, H. Gruber has shown that Darwin took a long time to recognize certain consequences that were implied with necessity by his previous statements.

As for the hypothesis of variable strength inherent in different forms of necessity, this is a delicate problem whose solution requires, more than that of any other problem, a distinction between necessity as a state and the dynamic process that leads to necessity. In mathematics, it is customary to speak of structures as being more or less strong or weak: a group is stronger than a monoid, and a field is stronger than a group. But does this mean simply that the stronger structures comprise a greater number of necessary relations—that is, that they are "richer"—or does it mean that the necessity of these relations is itself stronger in the twofold sense of more elaborated (=deeper reasons) and more amplified (more consequences and tighter mutual connections)? If we compare the analytical necessity of identity $(n=n)$ with the synthetic necessity of $n \rightarrow n+1$ (each whole number is succeeded by another whole number), it is clear that, once they are acquired, the two kinds of necessity impose themselves with the same compelling evidence. However, from the point of view of processes (necessitation), it is just as clear that the latter is richer in reasons and in consequences. If one accepts the close association between necessity and integration, the sense of "richer" is not only numerical but also implies a greater strength of integration, hence of operational synthesis. This, therefore, constitutes a factor to be considered in the evolution of necessitating processes.

On the other hand, there seems to be no basis for distinguishing a procedural from a structural kind of necessity. A procedure (including an operation seen as a particular activity occurring in a particular place and at a particular time) is aimed at success, not at comprehension. A procedure can succeed in providing sufficient, but nonnecessary conditions: for example, to correct a sequence 3,2,2 in the construction of slopes, as seen in chapter 4, it is not necessary to replace it by 4,3,2; it is sufficient to change its lowest level to obtain 3,2,1. But if necessity plays a part in a proedural behavior, which is usually the case, it is in terms of comprehending the reasons for success and failure, rather than at the level of the results as such. The reasons lead us to structural considerations from which procedures cannot be dissociated, except in the case of purely empirical, trial-and-error procedures.

V

As for the relations between necessity and possibility, it is obvious that any form of necessity derives from possible compositions, which establish relations between possibilities as well as between possibilities and actualized realities. Reciprocally, co-necessities generate new possibilities. Since both possibility and necessity are a product of the subject's activity rather than observables given by experience, it is natural that there be interdependencies between the two.

Putting aside the sensorimotor levels and considering only representational conceptualizations, we can distinguish three stages in the development of necessity. The first, which corresponds to the preoperational levels, is that of *pre-necessities*, which are local and incomplete. We have observed these in each of our preceding studies, as well as the pseudonecessities to which we shall return. The second stage, which goes together with the concrete operations, is that of limited co-necessities: the prefix *co-* means that they are jointly constituted and may form compositions with each other. They are limited in that they are applied or attributed to concrete contents only. At the hypothetico-deductive level, finally, one can speak of unlimited co-necessities that can be used in any formal deduction whatsoever.

These three stages correspond to those that we have established with respect to possibilities. To the first correspond the possibilities generated by analogical successions. These are few in number and poorly diversified because subjects content themselves with prolonging a few variations or actualizations that they just performed or noted in reality. At the second stage are constituted the concrete and limited co-possibilities, and at the third appear the co-possibilities of indefinite intension and unlimited extension; subjects at this level spontaneously speak of "infinities."

Thus, there are close parallels between the development of possibility and of necessity and, moreover, a definite relationship with that of the operational structures. But the latter are not what give direction to this development. Insofar as possibilities express differentiations and necessities express integrations, the origin of the operations is to be sought in the union of the two; if, on the other hand, one wished to attribute to them a primitive rather than a derived formative capacity, it would be difficult to see how the internalization of actions would be sufficient to furnish the well-structured, reversible structures that characterize the operational systems, or how possibility and necessity might get constituted even before the actions become internalized—that is, at a time when they appear in admittedly impoverished forms that are nevertheless rich in exactable developments.

Let us then examine their formation, assuming that stage-by-stage correspondence already intervenes at their inception. From this point of view, it would be totally erroneous to assume an initial state constituted only by "reality," perceived as such in a pure state without connections to the subject, to which would be added, somewhat later, the joint construction of necessities and possibilities. Reality being, right from the beginning, assimilated to the subject's schemata, the initial states are characterized by a general lack of differentiation between reality, necessity, and possibility. On the one hand, given the impoverished state in number and structure of the elementary assimilatory schemata, reality is perceived as being the way it "must be," which leads to generalized pseudonecessity.* On the other hand, the only possibilities are the few variations the subject actually perceives. This initial undifferentiated state is then followed, in a series of steps, by the emergence of differentiation between the three modalities; but many residues of the initial fusion remain, in the first of our stages, in the form of pseudonecessities and the restriction of possibilities to those actually realized.

What, then, is the common origin of necessities and possibilities as they become differentiated from their initial fusion with reality? The answer is simple. It is not to be found in reality as such, objectively external to the subject, since reality is only what it is and the observable facts that can be registered do not contain in themselves either possibilities or necessities. Rather, the latter have their source, naturally, in the increasing number of assimilatory schemata and their reciprocity, which become coordinated and lead to the development of inferential capacities. The coordination of the schemata leads to compositions that generate prenecessities and local necessities that replace the initial, generalized pseudonecessity. However, any given composition also suggests other possible ones. Finally, external, exogenous reality becomes inserted within these new relationships of emerging necessities and possibilities and becomes more objective, giving rise to questions of why, how, and, in general, to questions of comprehension.

VI

Returning to the role of necessity and possibility in the formation of operations, we are not concerned with explaining the constitution of an isolated operation, such as the union or intersection of classes, but with accounting for the essential characteristic of any kind of operation that aggregates systems containing three

---

*This perception can even be found in prescientific theories in the history of physics. R. Garcia shows, in our book on the relations between psychogenesis and the history of science, that the physics of Aristotle constitutes an admirably constructed and coherent system whose only flaw is that, instead of starting from transformational premises, he based all his deductions on observables, which he considered intrinsically necessary—in other words, on pseudonecessities. J. Piaget and R. Garcia, *Psychogenèse et histoire des sciences* (Paris: Flammarion, 1983).

levels of organization—that of the whole, the parts or subsystems, and the elements created by particular operations or their products. This organization seems to be related to fairly well-understood mechanisms, such as reflecting abstraction and completive generalizations, that can explain the transition from relatively impoverished to richer structures. If one compares these developments with those of a living organism, one might (remaining at a fairly general level) make an analogy between these mechanisms and the so-called organizers that operate in the formation of "organs," which would correspond to the "structures" that cognition as a whole has at its disposal.

But to consider things from the other end—in comparing, for instance, the embryogenesis in primates or hominids with that of a larva in lower animals—a more general problem arises, which is that of the general directions that characterize what some contemporary biologists call "progress." This question also arises in genetic epistemology when we ask ourselves what the general functional processes are that seem to control these uninterrupted structural developments, on the level of the history of science as well as of psychogenesis in its sequence of stages.

To speak only of the functional aspects of transitions from a lesser structure to a more evolved one (a function may be fulfilled or exercised by the most diverse types of structural mechanisms or organs, such as assimilation), we see that they apparently consist in more and more diversified differentiations and integrations. Moreover, one of the three main forms of equilibration of cognitive structures is that of interactions between differentiation and integration. We have already referred to the interdependence of possibilities and necessary relations. Put differently, possibilities are the source of openings and necessity is the source of closures. The constant alternation of closures with new openings is likewise an essential characteristic of the integrated process that we are talking about. In short, necessitations and the formation of possibilities direct the whole process of structuring, but at a higher level.

VII

We now only need to situate reality with respect to these mechanisms—that is, the object as such, existing prior to knowledge, compared with what it becomes once it gets encompassed within the framework of necessities and possibilities constructed by the subject (without being modified, however, in its intrinsic characteristics, which remain independent of the subject). At first glance, reality may appear completely absorbed or "consumed" at its two ends by these constructions of the subject: at the start, it is reduced to nothing more than a particular case among other possible ones, and at the end, it finds itself subordinated to necessary ties. But, in either case, it becomes much richer by being better understood and promoted from the lower rank of an observable to the higher rank of reality interpreted. Two ambiguities still need to be cleared up.

The first would be to see a certain form of idealism in this subordination of reality to the subject's cognitive tools. But this would be completely false: in fact, the subject as an organism and source of material actions is also object (even when her actions become internalized as operations) and thus part of reality. This explains the surprising convergence of mathematics and physics.

The second ambiguity might result from the distinction we make between the object as it is and the object as interpreted by the subject. It would be to equate it with Kant's distinction between the *thing in itself* (noumenon) and the *thing as revealed* (phenomenon). But this would be equally false, since the subject in her cognitive activities comes to know and to reconstruct the object in increasingly adequate ways. However, every progress also opens up new problems so that the object becomes more and more complex and, in this sense, retreats as the subject approaches it. This means that the absolute difference between subject and object diminishes as a function of successive approximations. But there always remains a relative distance, with the object staying in a state of "limit," which is quite different from an unknowable and immutable noumenon.

What is to be learned from these situations is rather obvious: there exists no more an absolute beginning in the development of possibilities than one can determine an absolute end to necessity. Any necessity remains conditional and will need to be transcended. Thus, there do not exist any apodictic judgments that are intrinsically necessary.

Index

Index

Swiss-born psychologist **Jean Piaget** (1896–1980) taught at the Universities of Geneva and Lausanne. Among his many books published in English are *Language and Thought of the Child; The Moral Judgment of the Child; Play, Dreams, and Imitation; The Construction of Reality in the Child;* and *The Origins of Intelligence in Children.*

Translator **Helga Feider** earned a Ph.D. in linguistics at Indiana University in 1969, and is a professor in the department of psychology at the Université du Québec à Montréal.